CREATIVE CAREERS

UNLOCKING ART SCHOOL ADMISSIONS

A PARENT'S TOOLKIT FOR ART COLLEGE

Creative Careers
Unlocking Art School Admissions
A Parent's Toolkit for Art College

ISBN: 9781068719400 Paperback

Published by: Inspired By Publishing

The strategies in this book are presented primarily for enjoyment and educational purposes. Every effort has been made to trace copyright holders and obtain their permission for the use of copyright material.

The information and resources provided in this book are based upon the authors' personal experiences. Any outcome, income statements or other results, are based on the authors' experiences and there is no guarantee that your experience will be the same. There is an inherent risk in any business enterprise or activity and there is no guarantee that you will have similar results as the author as a result of reading this book.

The author reserves the right to make changes and assumes no responsibility or liability whatsoever on behalf of any purchaser or reader of these materials.

ACKNOWLEDGEMENTS

I'd like to express my gratitude to everyone who has inspired and supported me in creating this book.

First, thanks to the many parents who have trusted in my knowledge and expertise to guide their young people in following their creative dreams. Working with hundreds of creative students has been an absolute pleasure. Their experiences have given me valuable insights into the challenges of transitioning from school to college and university art and design courses. Every encounter offers me an opportunity to grow and refine my approach–the ultimate inspiration to write this book.

Although it was difficult, I appreciate my teenage self for the experiences that allowed me to solidify and share the understandings in this book with a wider audience.

I am also grateful to my amazing publishing team for keeping me on track and providing the structure my creative mind needs. Their feedback has been invaluable in ensuring this book came to life.

To my parents, thank you for always supporting my wish to study art, no matter how difficult it might have been.

Lastly, to my partner Neil for his unwavering support in everything I do. Also, to our teenage daughter, who inspires us every day to do better for young people. Thank you for your love, support and inspiration.

CONTENTS

INTRODUCTION

This is not your usual parenting book.

I'm not going to tell you what I think you probably want to hear – that if your young person works hard, and gets an A in their art class, that they're going to get their dream offer at university/art school.

Now that would be way too predictable!

However, this news is frustrating and seems very unfair – to all involved.

The art and design world IS unpredictable; however, this is the beauty of creativity and what we're here to unpack.

The sad fact is that there are many gifted potential artists who, if they had the support they needed whilst studying, would be out there making a huge difference in the cultural art and design industries today.

But they never really understood what it took to create that winning application, and they didn't realise the benefits of a creative education in the broader picture.

And I don't want your young person to be one of them.

My guess is that you're a parent, guardian or primary caregiver, and you're here reading this book because you're feeling lost and/or out of your depth, in an area that isn't your forte. When you're managing a teenager (or two or three), your own career and life, and possibly your own older parents, it can seem all a bit too much to handle. Who said kids get easier as they get older? It just gets different as I well know, with our own teenage daughter.

By the way, this may also be applicable to you if you're someone who is accountable for a young adult, whether by biological, legal or relational ties. This book is absolutely for you.

You're going to learn about the thinking and the mentality that underpins the creative world, how your young person can foster this, and how learning these skills now rather than later is going to set them up for life, not just the following year or so.

I'm going to take you through clear steps that guide you through the timeline of your young person having made the decision that they wish to apply to an art and design course at university, to the end, where they will be accepting their offer(s).

We'll look at where your young person currently is in their learning and what the possible journey could look like – there is usually more than one option.

Being successful with your portfolio is about the speed of implementation, and the sooner your young person starts, the more advanced their portfolio is likely to be.

Each chapter has suggestions on how to take action to encourage your young person to view their art practice outside the school curriculum. Additionally, they are guided to see it as an intrinsic part of who they are.

I'm aiming to bring awareness to the differences between what your young person is doing at school to excel, and what they need to be doing to make the transition successfully to university.

Therefore, I've written the book that I guess my parents wished they'd had when I didn't get into art school for the first time when I was 18.

With the challenges of modern life playing havoc with young people's mental health, I am going to encourage you and them to take steps, together if you wish, to embrace failure, to take more risks, to be more reflective and self-aware. This can help build resilience if only we can let ourselves. We, myself included, the teachers and schools, spend a lot of time seeking to avoid letting our young people fail; we love them, we care about their feelings and well-being.

But to be safe in the knowledge that some failure in life is a good thing opens us up to vulnerabilities that we may not know we have. However, by embracing this in the process and journey of creating, it can catapult a student to heights they never knew possible.

There's plenty that you as a parent can be doing to support your young person in this journey. And if you have awareness, it may well even influence you and *your* creativity.

I've had the experience of working with students and their art and design portfolios for university and art school since 2000. Eleven of those years have also involved a close relationship with parents in my freelance capacity.

I've talked to parents who struggle with many aspects of the art and design educational experience and lifestyle. However, once *you* have more understanding of the underpinning processes, you will be able to recognise where your young person needs to focus and find the support that they need to enable their confidence to soar.

We'll not be covering practical, technical art and design-making skills – this is what they work hard on at school. What I'm here to provide is a glimpse into what you've perhaps never considered about HOW art and design are produced, and what mindset and critical thinking are involved.

I'd like to challenge your perceptions of what creativity is. Just this morning I was witness to a discussion among other mums around the notion of their teens being "good" at art. In this instance, they weren't! Their art was apparently still at a level of drawings of stick people – using this as a benchmark for talent.

Throughout the book, we'll keep in mind that each young person is an individual, and the process and timescale will reflect this. What might be right for one may not be for others. It's a recognition of this individuality that will be intrinsically linked to your young person's success. Ultimately, my main approach is to encourage you and them to *exploit* their individuality – those differences and quirks, if demonstrated, are highly regarded at the universities.

I'm sure you've likely spent a lot of time with your young person researching the process of applying to university and the various courses. My experience is that parents often may not feel any better informed – just more confused with the myriad of information that all sounds alike, yet different.

I aim to demystify the language and intent of the information you'll find on the internet. In the section on the content of your young person's application, we'll deep-dive into more practical elements of the Universities and Colleges Admissions Service (UCAS) application, personal statement, references, and of course, the all-important portfolio and interview. This, I hope, will prepare you both for the road ahead, that, with the right knowledge, can be a wonderful challenge; and without this knowledge, the road can be a minefield.

Sometimes the complexity of making the application for art and design courses at university just seems too complicated and overwhelming, therefore a change of direction is taken.

If there's one takeaway from this book that I'd like you to have, it is this:

I have met many adults who return to creative education, having spent years in a job that didn't fulfil them. They seek to start a creative degree because they weren't "allowed" in their teens, by parents who didn't support them for whatever reason. My experience is that if this strong desire to have a creative outlet is ignored, it will fester away until some action is taken. I recognise that pursuing dreams isn't always feasible, but by supporting and nurturing your young person's creative aspirations now, they will impact lives, including their own, in ways beyond your imagination.

Finally, I understand that having a creative teen can pose all kinds of challenges. It can be the mess, the disorganisation, the late-night inspired sessions, the uncertainty about their career, all of which may be totally outside of your comfort zone.

It's common that dyslexia is also thrown into the mix, but ultimately this *can* be their strength. Many dyslexic individuals possess the advantageous quality of thinking outside the box, often generating innovative and profitable ideas, which is a great contribution when working as part of a creative team.

Additionally, some dyslexics demonstrate adeptness in logical reasoning, showcasing their skills as fabulous critical thinkers – a valued skill to possess when working within the creative process.

Art and design serve as a vital aspect of global culture, influencing political discourse and providing a safe place amidst adversity. It affords individuals a refuge during times of distress, fostering a sense of recognition in an otherwise challenging world.

Additionally, art and design enable us to enhance our existence in ways that bring joy, countering darkness. Can you even imagine a world devoid of literature, music, cinema, artistic expression, fashion, architectural wonders, and interior design?

The creative need in all of us to make something from nothing, creation itself, enriches existence, bringing vibrancy and motivation to life.

Imagine seeing your young person gain the offers at university, but more importantly, the confidence and personal fulfilment to continue their journey in life with integrity to who they are and what they stand for. That's all a parent could ever ask for.

There are additional resources for you to download and use to assist you in making the most of this book.

You can download them here:
www.portfolio-oomph.com/creativecareers

'Drawing is 90% looking,
10% doing."

Peter Prendergast, Painter

1

Where Are You At?

Step One: Get the Facts
Step Two: Mind the Gap

Where Are You At?

1

In order to know where we're going, it is important to understand our starting point.

And when applying to university to study art and design, it's important to know where we are right now.

Your young person might be in one of a number of positions that will affect their journey and the processes that they undertake.

Your young person might have had very clear ideas about wanting to study art from early on in high school.

Or maybe like me, they're just falling into it, because, really, nothing else speaks to them. This is common and absolutely nothing out of the ordinary.

Something that I believe differs with our young people and their education compared to our own, is this expectation that they should know what career it is that they wish to follow while they are still at school.

However, the creative world is much more ambiguous than most career paths, and jobs are much less well-known about. Also, many opportunities in the arts are for the self-employed, and the concept of portfolio careers is more common, as opposed to traditional "jobs" as such. This can be a difficult way of life to grasp if your experience has been a job for life.

Because I wasn't really interested in anything at school other than art and design, I just followed what was expected of me: Do A levels, then a foundation course, then a degree. However, I had to study other subjects at A level that I didn't really enjoy, to fill my timetable. I failed them, so for me, this wasn't the best scenario.

Of course, there were options after O levels before embarking on my A levels, aged 16, but I didn't know about this. Neither did my parents, nor was it suggested at school. In hindsight I would have loved to have studied a more focused art and design pathway earlier on, however I was quite young for my age and this was unknown – also because no one else at school knew either!

I firmly believe that university isn't the only way, and it's not always the right way for everyone, especially considering the amount of debt that can be accrued in the process.

This is a great path to observe, and is how student Niamh reached her goals by taking bold action when she knew what she needed to do.

Niamh's mum approached me, knowing that school wasn't providing the best environment for her daughter. Her options were to consider further education as soon as her Higher exams were over (Highers are the exams that students aged 16 to 18 in Scotland sit that qualify for university and further study). The route that she took was to leave school at 16 and study UAL Level 3 Diploma in Art and Design, instead of the usual Scottish system route of staying on at school until 6th year for Advanced Highers.

This Diploma year led nicely to securing a place at Duncan of Jordanstone College of Art and Design (DJCAD, part of Dundee University). The final episode, for now, was studying for a Masters in Children's Book Illustration at Cambridge School of Art.

So you can see that Niamh could have stayed on at school to study the Advanced Higher, and it MAY have taken her to apply for university the following year. However, depending on where students are aiming for, it's my view that the Advanced Highers don't always give the competitive edge that is required. Attending college to focus on art and design earlier can be the stronger option, though it's very much dependent on the individual and the school.

It's important that you know what the options are earlier rather than later, as being in an environment where your young person doesn't feel that they "fit" can be very demotivating. It can also be quite detrimental to their mental health if they feel they are being shoehorned into an educational experience where they are getting very little satisfaction or being able to express themselves within the curriculum.

This can save a lot of stress on everyone's part if school isn't really the best place for your young person – for whatever reason.

Get this element of the planning right, and you'll have a young person who is excited about their creativity. They will feel fulfilled by the creative challenges they face and are stretched to learn and grow as an artist or designer.

There is the notion that to attend university or art school, a student needs to have completed an art qualification at A level, Higher, etc. A student studying for an International Baccalaureate that doesn't contain art will also be feeling somewhat disadvantaged. However, with hard work and some expert support, your young person *can* succeed in their quest, even if they aren't studying art at school. Remember, the road to success is varied, and as they say, "There are many ways to skin a cat".

I've worked with three students who recently left school without art or design as a qualification, and all three went on to excel in their chosen fields.

Take Claudia. She'd already left school without studying Art at Higher level. We were working together on her portfolio, and she had registered with the local school for her to achieve the Higher Art, as that was what she'd understood was required. The possibilities within the prescriptive Scottish Qualifications Authority (SQA) curriculum were hampering her confidence and interest. Therefore, we took a chance because she was qualified with the number of other Highers, at the grades required, to drop this exam and focus on the portfolio. The change in motivation and focus from this decision was astounding – she began to apply herself in a manner that I hadn't seen before.

You can see that it really does depend very much on circumstances, where a student focuses their energies, and seeking advice can make all the difference.

Leaving school before the more advanced years can be an advantage for some students. College has a slightly different atmosphere to it compared to school. There is an expectation that you'll be a little more self-motivated, and it somehow just seems more of a mature environment.

I had a student many years ago tell me that their guidance teacher at school had told her that she was way too clever to go to college and not university.

Which wasn't helpful, considering she'd not got into university, did this make her not clever enough? Incidentally, she went on to study a Foundation course at college and subsequently skyrocketed into second-year university, excelled, and achieved a first-class honours degree. She is now a very successful illustrator.

Therefore the notion that only moving on to university from school is a credible route is not in the students' best interests. It also shows a lack of understanding of how the visual arts education journey differs from that of academic subjects.

If you're a parent who is not involved in the creative world, the possibilities can seem a very daunting procedure. And you may compare this to a student who is applying for History, English or languages for example, where they apply to university and are offered a place – based solely on exam results.

So by the end of this Chapter, you will understand the education options available for your young person in the visual arts, based on their current stage in life or education.

Step One: Get The Facts

To understand the options for your young person, you need to gather facts based on what they are currently studying, or what qualifications they already have if they're not studying.

What is the highest qualification that your young person holds? Or if they are still studying, what is the qualification they are currently studying for, and what are their predicted grades/outcomes?

Start with a good old online search into your local college's courses, in the art and design area. Add to this the university courses that your young person is interested in.

For the courses that sound interesting, make a note of the entrance qualifications. Is this in line with what they are currently studying for, or the qualifications that they currently hold? If your young person is currently studying for the exams that are required by the university or college, are their predicted grades high enough?

If your young person is on track to achieve the grades to get into university, then all is good. However, I also advise having a backup plan for further education college, if the grades aren't achieved.

When looking at further education college courses, observe what the progression route is – it may be another higher level course at the same college, an "Higher National Certificate / Diploma (HNC/D), for example, or it may be going into a degree course. There are also courses that lead into industry/employment in the design areas.

This gives you and your young person a strong basis from which to make the best decision the first time round.

If you don't get this right, you may find that your young person starts a course that is too low a level, and they feel frustrated and unmotivated, that they are spending time repeating lots of what they've already done at school. This can lead to dropping out when a student doesn't see a clear reason or challenge in what they're doing.

STEP TWO: Mind The Gap

Other than your young person's academic qualifications, what evidence is needed to get onto the course of their choice?

If your young person is qualified (or will be, once they've finished their exams) for the course that they wish to apply for, then Chapter 4 on the application process will inform you on how to apply.

If this research isn't done early, you can end up in a situation that a parent I had helped found themselves in. Their teenage son had wanted to apply for art at university, but he had thought he didn't need a portfolio. They had visited the Open Days together, and the realisation that a portfolio was needed was quite a shock, and panic ensued. It had also been emphasised that a portfolio shouldn't contain schoolwork alone – but work done outside of school. We'll go more into portfolios, what they are, and if your young person will indeed need one, in Chapter 6 on Content.

Somewhere in the planning at school, either with the teachers or in the communication with the parents, this vital piece of information was lost.

And sometimes we only hear what we want to hear, as we all know.

Therefore, if you, the parent, are organised, and you know to expect that lines of communication between school, young person, and yourself can become a bit hazy, you'll have a clear idea of what the reality is and what the facts are.

Your Tasks

- Note where your young person is in terms of qualifications they hold or are studying for.
- Research online on the art and design courses at university and college fully. By this, I mean to visit the institution's website for up-to-date information regarding what their entrance requirements are. This information is usually on the main pages of each subject. However, if your young person is applying from outside the country they are applying, you'll need to research the grade requirements for their current exam system in that particular country.
- Make a note of the courses that your young person is/will be qualified for. Check out the progression routes from these courses to see if they match with expectations. Failing to do this stage can result in finding out that the course you studied perhaps at further education does not lead you into a degree programme – if that's your ultimate goal.
- It's also beneficial at this stage to note what supplementary materials they need to provide in terms of portfolio, interview etc.

2

What Do You Want to Be?

2

What Do You Want to Be?

In the years that I interviewed students at Edinburgh College of Art for entrance into the first year, I became quite surprised at the number of students who asked about career options following their years in university.

And understandably so. As the cost of living has soared, this particular question has become a very real concern for some: How might we find ourselves earning money in the future?

For others, just the instinct of following their passions and strengths is enough to know that they'll make it work if they stay true to themselves.

When I applied to art college in the early 1990s for Fine Art printmaking, I genuinely didn't give a moment's thought to what I would be doing after I graduated. In hindsight this was a good thing, but also possibly a bad thing.

I was very fortunate that my parents didn't seem too concerned, and they were happy to support me in following a course of study that really excited me.

I do remember having a mini meltdown on my foundation course where I genuinely couldn't see what I would be doing after studying art and design. I visited the careers service in Derby, and if I'm honest, that was of little help. The only option they could offer as a possibility was to work at Sotheby's auction house.

And guess what? That wasn't really what I wanted to be doing.

After three years, I graduated in 1994 with a degree in Fine Art printmaking. While I was on this course, there were no discussions around our employability and transferable skills. We were given no professional development, and by that I mean we weren't prepared for work after our degree.

A large part of operating successfully as an artist is having the ability to promote and market yourself, run a business, and find multiple income streams. I believed that I had a degree in printmaking, and therefore I was qualified to print. That's all.

All rather limiting in today's world.

Thankfully, things have moved on significantly in education, the jobs market and opportunities since 1994.

The world has opened up with the Internet, home working, Zoom, Teams etc., and the possibilities for graduates these days are immense. Never have we been able to network so easily using social media platforms like LinkedIn and Instagram. Nor have we been able to promote ourselves, our art and design products, and our services online as easily through platforms like Etsy, Behance, The Dots, our own website, and through online galleries.

Therefore, as with any career choice, finding your market, which may be global, is so much easier, and opportunities so much more vast.

The Creative Industries

The creative industries are vital to our economy. At the time of writing this book in 2024, the United Kingdom employs over two million people in this field, and its growth is much faster than others. According to recent statistics from the Department for Digital, Culture, Media & Sport (DCMS) they contributed £109 billion to the economy in 2021. This equated to 5.6% of the total for that year. This is largely due to developments in digital technologies, and the game and film industries.

I think the biggest misconception of the value and purpose of arts education is this:

> **"The true purpose of arts education is not necessarily to create more professional dancers or artists. It's to create more complete human beings who are critical thinkers, who have curious minds, who can lead productive lives."**
>
> Kelly Pollock – Former Executive Director at the COCA (Centre of Creative Arts Missouri)

We mustn't view creative degrees as only preparing a young person for a particular job. There are of course some jobs that creative degrees lead directly into. However, there is a high chance that your young person will become a freelancer or self-employed, and they will be their own boss and create their own job.

In a world where life is complex and problems are needing to be solved to meet rapid changes in life, creative thinking is a hugely valuable asset.

Nurses do it. Engineers do it. So do teachers. And even those from the

Financial sector do it.

The Value of Creative Thinking

Because creative thinking is a skill required in all professions, art-and design-trained individuals are of high value to any team. For a student who studies in the creative industries, it is possible that postgraduate study might take them in a side step to further their training to a more specific career route.

In The Future of Jobs Report 2023 by the World Economic Forum,

> "Analytical thinking and creative thinking remain the most important skills for workers in 2023. Analytical thinking is considered a core skill by more companies than any other skill and constitutes, on average, 9% of the core skills reported by companies. Creative thinking, another cognitive skill, ranks second, ahead of three self-efficacy skills – resilience, flexibility and agility; motivation and self-awareness; and curiosity and lifelong learning – in recognition of the importance of workers' ability to adapt to disrupted workplaces."

Wherever Artificial Intelligence (AI) takes us, and in particular the creative industries, there will need to be great collaboration between artists and regulators to agree on best practices around AI. This is an area to keep abreast of, as with any career. There has been much research done around the risk levels of different career routes comparing the probability of AI taking over. For example, Fashion Design is estimated to be a 13% risk, and Interior Design a 0% risk; whereas Accountancy is at 71% risk. Technology is constantly evolving, and this is an area to remain vigilant of.

The Skills They Don't Explicitly "Teach"

What I'd like to highlight here is my discovery, many years after graduation: the concept of transferable and employability skills.

These are very much buzzwords, but by ignoring what you're *actually* doing other than the technical skills during a creative degree, you're really rendering it far less valuable.

The University of Winchester provided a list of many of the transferable skills that your young person will learn and use day in and day out during their creative education. These skills are useful in any career, as we've mentioned previously, and by harnessing and acknowledging these skills, we become much more attractive both as employees and as independent self-employed entrepreneurial artists and designers. I've adapted this list based on what I've experienced with many young adults.

Employability and Transferable Skills For Your Young Person

Playing with possibilities: *How willing are you to try out new and different ways of expressing yourself?*

Making connections: *How good are you at linking different techniques, experiences and ideas?*

Using intuition: *How good are you at "having a hunch" about something?*

Wondering and questioning: *How much do you think about the world around* *you, and also the work you and others produce?*

Exploring and investigating: *How willing are you to try out new and different techniques and ideas?*

Challenging assumptions: *How willing are you to challenge something which you are told is correct?*

Tolerating uncertainty: *How easily do you find it not to be sure about something you do?*

Sticking with difficulty: *How well do you stick at something when you are finding it difficult?*

Daring to be different: *How easy do you find it to go your own way and be different from the crowd?*

Sharing the product: *How easy do you find it to share your work with others?*

Giving and receiving feedback: *How easy do you feel about others talking about your work and you talking about the work of others?*

Cooperating appropriately: *How easy do you find it being part of a team?*

Reflecting critically: *How often do you think about your work in a reflective, critical manner? Are you overly critical as regards your own work?*

Developing techniques: *How easy do you find it to acquire the basics of a new technique?*

Crafting and improving: *Once you have the basics of a new technique, how easy do you find it to develop your skills?*

You'll also notice from the list above that there are many life skills that your young person will be learning, practising and refining whilst in a creative education.

Tolerating uncertainty is surely essential in modern life, as the rapid rate of change is sometimes very challenging. As Tony Robbins once said,

> **"The quality of your life is in direct proportion to the amount of uncertainty you can comfortably deal with."**

By wondering and questioning, exploring and investigating, and challenging assumptions, we're thinking creatively, open to all options. These are very highly valuable skills.

You can download the full illustration of the Employability and Transferable Skills in the resources area at www.portfolio-oomph.com/creative careers.

Employment

Of course, many creative careers *are* in direct line with a particular course at university. For example, if your young person is interested in applying for costume design, then they will have ambitions to work within theatre and the thriving TV and film industry, which have exploded in recent years thanks to lockdowns and streaming platforms like Netflix, etc.

Your young person may want to study jewellery design, and of course, their ambition will be to be a jeweller. The likelihood that they'll be self-employed, creating their own creative pieces, is highly probable. I would say that there aren't that many "jobs" as jewellers, so having an entrepreneurial spirit and developing the skills to run their own creative business are critical.

Now, if I consider my peers from my fine art printmaking degree, the jobs that we have found ourselves in are varied: members of academia, a photographer for Visit Scotland, primary and secondary school art teachers, art conservationist, practising artist, website designer, to name a few.

Bands are sometimes formed at art school too. From my time in Dundee, painting graduate Tom Simpson went on to join Snow Patrol in the late 90's and noughties. Fine Art graduate Aaron Garbut went on to be instrumental in the Rockstar North company, with the Grand Theft Auto game.

These examples were both formed from connections made whilst on these creative courses. And as you can see, our paths have led to all manner of careers.

For your young person to obtain an idea of some of the employment opportunities that lead from studying art and design, you can download the Creative Pathways document in the resources area at www.portfolio-oomph.com/creativecareers.

This list is not exhaustive – the website Prospects (www.prospects.ac.uk) is also a great website that offers extensive information about careers in the Creative Industries.

Being a Freelance Artist or Designer

You may have heard of the term "portfolio careers" – this is very common in the creative industries.

That means they are earning a living from working with different clients, on a range of projects and revenue streams. It is therefore essential to be able to manage one's own time, selling products, soliciting services, and finding ways to pay the bills.

This is a very different way of living compared to other sectors and goes against what has been the norm until recent years. Jobs for life are becoming fewer, and this offers great variety – but also uncertainty.

Artists will do a range of tasks within their practice, aside from making art. They will exhibit and negotiate with galleries, write project proposals and funding applications, curate, work in academia perhaps, present papers at conferences, give talks, run workshops, sell and market themselves. As such, they'll also need a keen eye for their finances as a self-employed person and submitting tax returns, etc.

You can see that life can be very varied and many skills do need to be developed to create success.

My personal opinion is that an artist or maker needs to commit to the notion that only 50% of their time will be spent on making. The other 50% needs to be devoted to a clear, targeted marketing/self-promotion strategy. I've witnessed many incredibly talented artists and makers who are either unwilling or unable to commit to or accept this. As a consequence, they really struggle to make a success of their art as a career.

Understandably, it is difficult bigging yourself up. But there are other ways to do this, i.e., galleries are in a position to represent artists to initiate the sales. Ultimately you do need to be able to big yourself up to the galleries!

So what does this changing landscape mean for your creative teen?

It can seem rather daunting when pathways to economic stability and successful careers aren't clear. The answers are muddy and vary across professions.

If your young person does decide they wish to become an artist, sometimes there is a need to combine creative work with other employment – to provide some stability.

However, this also might provide inspiration for their work and fulfil aspects of their needs that aren't provided for by working alone in a studio.

I would say that becoming an artist or designer is very much a lifestyle. If you find yourself as a parent who has worked in a steady job for life in a very different field, with a teenager wishing to study art and design, you might find this quite a frightening prospect.

I've met many parents in this position. By embracing the mindset that we'll discuss later in Chapter 5, alongside skills in the previous list, the creative industries can provide a nourishing environment in which creatives can thrive.

There are challenges as with any career – however, my view is that we are only on this planet once. And as Mark Twain has famously said,

> **"Find a job you enjoy doing, and you will never have to work a day in your life."**

So considering what we've discussed in this Chapter on careers, is your creative teen aware of the tenacity, resilience and self-motivation required to not only succeed in the creative industries but also to thrive?

Given that the school experience in art and design is very limited, have they realised the full extent of the possible careers within the creative industries that they perhaps have no experience of yet?

It's important that they realise that if they have only really done art involving painting and drawing at school, there may be many other avenues in terms of careers that they could align with. And this can be explored early on before making choices about which degree to specialise in. The previous Chapter will come into play here as a Foundation course is a real game changer in giving students great realisations about where their skills and interests lie.

Your Tasks

Ask your young adult these questions and give them an opportunity to reflect on the type of career they may be interested in:

- Do you like working on a brief set by someone else? A client for example. This will help your young person to see that as a designer, many projects are set by a client. It's not exclusive to designers, as fine artists sometimes work to commission, however in many cases, this can help to narrow down a focus.

- Are they interested in working 2 dimensionally or 3 dimensionally? This can help decide between careers in both the art and design areas. For example, 3D areas would be sculpture in the fine arts and jewellery in the design area. Compare this to 2D practises of painting and printmaking in the fine arts and illustration in the design area.

- What materials do they enjoy working with? This is broad and doesn't really define a possible career as such. However, it's useful if a student particularly enjoys working with fabrics for example, then fashion, textiles, and performance costume would all be possible careers. If they enjoy working in wood it could be furniture design, product design or fine art sculpture that interests them.

Doing their research about possible careers and seeing how a range of artists and designers work can really influence which subject they go on to choose to study for their specialism.

One final word: Doing a degree in one subject does not commit you to a lifetime career in that area! Remember those transferable skills? ALL creative courses use ALL those skills. Therefore movement, side steps and outright changes in career can and do happen.

How exciting, let's get started!

3

What Is Creativity (And What's The Issue)?

Creativity in School
Creativity Post-School
Permission to Fail
Quantity Over Quality

3 What *Is* Creativity (And What's The Issue)?

Creativity is spoken about in many scenarios, and it's my belief that it can be very nuanced.

It is vital therefore to understand what is meant by the word creativity in the context of art and design at further and higher education levels.

There was a parent who contacted me with a problem that summarises perfectly a common issue with school work.

Emily's mum Sally had noticed that throughout Emily's school years, it became apparent that she enjoyed art and had a talent for it. However, she really lacked confidence. She was academic and was getting good grades in all subjects and thought it safer and less scary to write essays rather than expose herself as an artist.

"Before really connecting with her creativity, Emily was happy drawing, painting but she was not creating. She clearly had the skills but was copying from photos, paintings, etc. Although her teachers were very encouraging, they weren't helping her think for herself."

Sally knew that there was something missing in the work: that Emily wasn't expressing herself, and her personality was not coming through in her work. This knocked her confidence a bit.

Emily had a few frustrating months trying to find a voice and be inspired on a personal level. She knew what she needed to do but found it difficult. But with guidance through this difficult process, Emily began to explore possibilities – both techniques and ideas. Gradually Emily found a strong theme to align with. Some things worked, some things didn't; but she was experimenting and had support to help her focus.

The portfolio that she presented for university was a million miles away from what she had previously been doing - she was accepted to her first choice university that year.

I agree with this quote from Robert E. Franken in *Human Motivation*, 3rd ed.:

> **"Creativity is defined as the tendency to generate or recognise ideas, alternatives, or possibilities that may be useful in solving problems, communicating with others, and entertaining ourselves and others."**

By failing to recognise this full definition, your young person is setting themselves up for disappointment. When their ability to render lifelike copies of photos isn't rewarded by the universities, it can be very difficult to understand what they are seeking in a portfolio.

Creativity in School

When we talk about creativity in many cases, we often refer to drawing or just the act of creating *something*. We interchange the technical skill of being able to reproduce an object in drawn, painted, sculpted or other form as being creative.

And much of the school curriculum rewards students for having strong technical ability to reproduce artists' work, objects, etc. into 2D or 3D forms. Sometimes this is done from life, often it is done from photographs.

Students need to understand the key concepts, the elements of art and foundational skills to be able to succeed in the school curriculum. And we start learning these from early on in our school experience. The elements of art are features that are included within an art piece to help the artist and designer to communicate effectively with their work. The seven most common elements include line, shape, texture, form, space, colour and value, with the additions of mark making, subject matter, composition, technique and materiality.

Ask a high school student about these skills and they may even have forgotten that they learnt them, because they'll be considering all these elements on autopilot, almost like riding a bike, without thinking.

The higher we go up in the school years, the greater emphasis is placed on using these in our work – and we're assessed against these criteria for a large part. So omitting these core foundational skills will result in lower grading exams, which is never a good thing, especially as entrance grades are so high for university.

Creativity Post-School

However, I have yet to see in a university's assessment criteria of a portfolio, a section that grades a student based on mastery of any of these aforementioned technical skills.

An area where students are not explicitly credited in their university application is their approach, which, in my opinion, results in greater creativity.

Universities seek exciting artwork in a portfolio that demonstrates experimentation, risk taking, failure and reflection upon this. This is where the value lies, and is what differentiates portfolios that are successful for university or art college from those that aren't.

Permission to Fail

If a student can embrace this "permission to fail", to make a mess, to make mistakes, then this allows them to think visually. This visual thinking is the basis for strong sketchbook work that demonstrates the developmental stages of a project.

In my experience, many students have many ideas of how they will approach a project/brief.

Students *think* about an idea and *think* it through…visualise it and often talk themselves out of it before they've even put pen or pencil to paper. Maybe they ask a friend or even you, their parent, what you think. But until it's actually out of their head and into a physical form, how can we judge whether this is a good idea or not?

Creative individuals can visualise these amazing ideas of what they want to make, but until they actually start to explore them visually, in reality then an idea can very quickly be dismissed – unless they're willing and able to accept that it might not be very good to begin with.

Accepting that it's an iterative process that requires revision, sometimes on a multitudinal scale, is essential.

Sir James Dyson made 5,127 prototypes before his bagless vacuum cleaner design came to life – five years after his initial idea.

However, it can be difficult to have the courage to put down ideas in physical form in case it's not "good enough". In case it's been done before. In case it goes wrong. In case we get judged. In case, in case.....(you fill in the blanks!)

Students I work with often get so stuck at this very early stage, and it really stops them even getting started. The fear of the blank white page is a real thing. It can make or break an application to university or art college.

There are many tried and tested ways that can be adopted to break down these barriers. Many of these "exercises" are done in the life drawing room as "warm ups". However they can be transferred to any type of drawing or project idea or brief.

- Drawing with the non-dominant hand
- Quick-timed drawings: Choose a range from 30 seconds to 5 minutes
- Drawing with a piece of charcoal or a pencil taped to the end of a garden cane: have their paper on the floor

All of the abovementioned exercises can be great fun, and the results unexpected. Our own expectation of a drawing done by any of these techniques is low due to the lack of control of our materials. We then start to see the marks and experience with a different lens when the mindset around "Is it good?" is not so valid.

I was quite surprised and delighted to hear how inspired one student and her family were enjoying some of the early elements of my portfolio preparation course.

Molly hadn't been successful in her applications the previous year. Consequently her confidence was low. Her mum Keren was keen to do all she could to help build Molly back up.

We talked about having fun with materials, playing and taking the pressure off from producing a final piece, to getting lost in the moments of creation that lead to final pieces.

Molly, Keren and Grandma all undertook the mark making experiences together, in the garden. They laughed, had fun together, explored new materials and limiting beliefs *together*, about art and creativity.

Molly has since received her dream offer, a place she never thought she'd conquer: Edinburgh College of Art (University of Edinburgh) for Art. If you as the parent can demonstrate some of this carefree attitude to learning, which, let's face it, as adults, it probably doesn't happen very often - we can lead by example and give our young person "permission".

By using a sketchbook effectively and annotating it with your thoughts and your reflection on your work, this starts to build a picture of what is going on in your head, how you're making decisions about what you're choosing to pursue, and what you're dismissing in the creative process.

There is also the need for an understanding that drawing can be many things, not only realistic representations of life-like objects.

I have collections of images on Pinterest covering many aspects of art and design. In this instance it would be helpful for you and your young person to engage with a broader context of drawing, and consider how they can use more experimentation and playfulness with their materials using this inspiration. You can find a link to my Pinterest drawing board in the resources area at www.portfolio-oomph.com/creativecareers.

A distinct example comes to mind of when our daughter was around 7 years old. She'd been having some fun with coloured felt tip pens on corrugated box cardboard. The piece of card was covered in multi coloured, layer upon layer of frantic expressive fun - she was very pleased with her work.

Of course, I encouraged her to take it into school to show the teacher, always aiming to push the boundaries! She didn't even manage to get as far as showing the teacher, before another child commented "That's not art, that's just a load of scribbles".

And sitting next to me now, aged 15, she said on reading this, "I wish I'd never taken it into school".

So, her enjoyment, fun, expression and play with the materials wasn't seen as being valid.

It wasn't this child's fault. It's how society moulds us, we learn from what we see and hear. If this child had seen any of Cy Twombly's work, their response might have been quite different! I challenge you to Google him.

Furthermore, there is also confusion about what drawing can *be*.

So, if we're confused about what creativity AND drawing are, then how can we ever expect to know what the universities and art colleges are looking to see?

Aside from drawing, art can be many things. The origin of inspiration isn't limited to still life, landscape, art-inspired or in the style of other artists. More and more, the universities and art colleges want to see *ideas*. They want to see something that you're interested in, that you're communicating – through your artwork.

This can come as quite a surprise, when students are so familiar with working from a still life or portrait – especially if they work predominantly from photos.

There's one TED talk where I always send students to: "Teaching art or teaching to think like artists" by Cindy Foley. You can watch the full video in the resources area at www.portfolio-oomph.com/creativecareers

The concepts in Cindy Foley's TED talk illustrate beautifully the issues we have when it comes to understanding art and what the universities are looking for.

Cindy discusses the disconnect between creativity and art education.

Our persistent need in art education is to be able to *recognise* a "thing". For it to be absolute or concrete. Standards in art education require us to be tested and assessed - for the learner to be wrong or to be right.

However when art is so nebulous, how can this be an effective way to assess? Schools are challenged to cultivate creativity due to this testing culture.

Therefore a shift in perception will give students and parents the courage to fully understand creativity, by focusing on three critical habits that artists employ:

1. comfort with ambiguity
2. idea generation
3. transdisciplinary research

When we talk about these habits that artists employ, they are similar to those employability and transferable skills from Chapter 2.

Quantity Over Quality?

In most things in life, we are taught quality over quantity.

However, in art and design, this can be said to be rather misleading and unhelpful in the creative process.

The American animator, writer and teacher Walt Stanchfield once said,

> **"We all have 10,000 bad drawings in us. The sooner we get them out the better."**

And this issue crops up every time I see a student who is working towards their high school exams. I was guilty of this 35 years ago, and I didn't see it myself either, way back then!

Students work TOO slow, they don't produce *enough* to allow themselves to produce the quality they are truly capable of. There is an unspoken correlation between the amount of time that it takes to produce a piece of work to the perceived quality of the work.

For my O level art, I selected a theme of metamorphosis. I carefully thought about what I could draw, that was one object changing into another.

A-ha! A pencil changing into a snake! I planned six or seven stages where a pencil gradually changed into a snake, each one with more and more snake and the pencil area became shorter. It was painstakingly painted in watercolour, repetitive and intricate. It took weeks. Oh, how I wish I had a photo to show you!

The technical skill in making the pencil look like a pencil, and the snake to look like a snake was intense. And I believed that this was all that really mattered. When my grade came through, of course, I was disappointed. But I never really understood what was lacking or how I could improve on this. And no, I didn't ask; of course I didn't!

But the speed of work was the main aspect that I remember. Because it was painstakingly intricate, progress was slow. Had I been able to play and experiment with a more carefree approach, I might have been able to push my ideas into some other place more exciting. By focusing on more playful and experimental *quantity*, I would have had more ideas and prototypes to choose from - therefore creating better *quality*.

Your Tasks

Get your young person started today by creating a menu of different types of drawings that they can do from the list earlier in this Chapter. Encourage them to see it as a fun time; see what happens and have some fun together.

- Drawing with the non-dominant hand
- Quick timed drawings - choose a range from 30 seconds to 5 minutes
- Drawing with a piece of charcoal or a pencil taped to the end of a garden cane - paper on the floor.

Why not get involved in this together like Molly did with her mum Keren?

And report back to me - share your experiences or photos of your work and tag me in them. I love to see how students are inspired!

Instagram: @portfoliooomph
Facebook: portfolio.oomph

I encourage students to use a reflection document to ask questions of themselves – HOW they felt about the work that they produced in these quick-fire, fun activities.

Reflecting will help them learn the value of working like this, and it will also provide insightful annotations that they can use in their sketchbook process. You can download the reflection document in the resources area at www.portfolio-oomph.com/creativecareers.

"We all have 10,000 bad drawings in us, the sooner we get them out the better."

Walt Stanchfield, Animator, Writer and Teacher

4

How Do You Get Your Art Degree?

Foundation Diploma Courses
HNC/D Courses
Other College Courses for 16 Up
Application Deadlines
Timelines and When to Get Started

How Do You Get Your Art Degree?

Considering that you and your young person have a sound understanding of where they are at *now*, in terms of their qualifications, we need to understand what the options are moving forward and what the journey looks like. And it's always best to do this with as little stress as possible.

Knowing where you are heading with your young person is essential because this determines a few elements.

Based on my 13 years of experience preparing students for university and further education courses in art and design, the biggest advantage for students is fully understanding the process and requirements well ahead of time.

This Chapter is designed to bring awareness to the process that your young person will need to go through to make and prepare a solid application for art and design subjects. We'll look at the processes required for courses at different types of educational institutions: further education and university.

We'll cover the timeline from first deciding to apply to art and design courses, through practical soul-searching, to meeting application deadlines.

Second to this is getting started early. Of course, talent comes into this equation, but no amount of talent outperforms a student who can't meet the deadlines and doesn't give themselves enough time to produce their best work.

To enable your young person to produce the strongest portfolio that they can, remember from the previous Chapter this requires risk taking and failure. They also need to give themselves plenty of time. This is one of the biggest mistakes that a student can make: that they rush the application procedure and their portfolio.

Applying for art and design courses, at university in particular, is a varied and complex procedure. Stress levels often run high, as it's a prolonged time of intense focus – think marathon rather than sprint!

Many students make it a family affair, with parents or carers providing pivotal support in many aspects of the application process. I understand not all applicants have this opportunity; however, whatever you can do to assist in managing this is most advisable.

In this Chapter we'll look at what you and your young person can be doing and when to get your ducks in a row, so to speak. It will make the process more manageable and enjoyable.

Let's look at what the options are for your young person now that you know what qualifications they hold or are currently studying for.

Foundation Diploma Courses

In England it's usual to study a Foundation Diploma locally at your further education college after A levels and then apply for a three-year degree course.

Some universities in England don't require applicants to have a Foundation Diploma course. However many do, and the benefits to it are hugely advantageous.

As I am writing this from my location just outside Edinburgh, it's important to understand that there are two different education systems in Scotland and the rest of the UK.

In Scotland, degrees are 4 years and students at school in Scotland are usually qualified after their Highers in S5 (year secondary 5). However, many go on to S6 year to gain more Highers and/or Advanced Highers.

Students in England wishing to apply to Scotland could apply straight from school to the university for what is a four-year degree course (bypassing a Foundation Diploma) – or if they choose to do a Foundation Diploma course, they will usually be qualified for direct entry into second year. This is what I did.

It's not uncommon for students in Scotland not to get into their chosen university straight from school. There are Foundation Diploma courses and portfolio preparation courses in Scotland, however please ensure that your young person is aware of the progression routes as we discussed in Chapter 1.

Some students see studying a Foundation Diploma as wasting time, when they could just be getting on with their degree. I do get it. Why "waste" a year?

However, a Foundation Diploma course is hugely advantageous when students working at school have a very limited experience of the different kinds of art and design. Studying in a Foundation Diploma course in no way reflects that a student isn't or wasn't good enough without one.

It's just that the narrow experience that some students have at school makes it very difficult to decide about which area is most suited for them to study.

The list below is not exhaustive, but it gives you a fair idea of the scope. Also, a young person at school will have had no experience of many of these specialisms, whilst some sound very similar to each other:

- Painting and Printmaking
- Drawing and Painting
- Sculpture
- Sculpture and Environmental Art
- Fine Art
- Printmaking
- Illustration
- Graphic Design / Communication
- Photography

- Film and TV
- Textiles
- Architecture
- Fashion Design
- Performance Costume Design
- Set Design
- Product Design
- Interior Design
- Jewellery Design

By getting into a Foundation Diploma course, your young person will experience many different design areas, from jewellery to illustration, textiles to performance costume for example. Also, they'll study in a far wider context across the different areas of the fine arts.

Additionally, a good Foundation Diploma course will also provide a different process experience. There's likely to be more emphasis on experimental work, risk taking and pushing the boundaries of the creative process than are likely to have been experienced at school.

I also firmly believe that a student gains more and will have a more valuable experience on their degree if they have studied a Foundation Diploma course first.

I studied a Foundation Diploma course after my A levels at the age of 18, feeling very unsure of my future and myself if I'm honest. I applied for degree courses expecting to get an offer because I'd been given no indication that my work was lacking in any area. However, the first year I applied I wasn't successful in securing a place anywhere.

I even went through UCAS Clearing (where all the unfilled spaces on courses across the UK become available and up for grabs).

Can you imagine?

I was gutted.

But in hindsight and all honesty, I didn't make the most of my Foundation Diploma. I failed to adequately embrace critical aspects of the process and mindset that really mattered. However, at the time I was blissfully unaware of any of this.

I found myself repeating the Foundation Diploma course – the penny dropped during this second year of what I was lacking. However, I feel it was also down to my immaturity mainly because I was one of the youngest in the school year cohort, and I believe that I just needed that extra time.

Even if your young person thinks they're ready to start a degree course, maybe emotionally they won't be. And perhaps they won't make the most of their experience if they skip the Foundation Diploma year.

When looking for a Foundation Diploma course, do ensure that it is accredited with progression routes in degree programmes.

If applying to a Foundation Diploma course, the application is made direct to the college not via the central body UCAS (we'll discuss this later). Many students apply to their local further education college or university, where a bursary or tuition fee funding may be available if you're under 19 years old.

It's possible to apply for as many courses at further education colleges as your young person wishes to.

They will be asked to complete their application form, including a written statement, submission of a portfolio (usually digital) and possibly an interview. Each college is different, so please do research this well.

However, if you're a Scottish student or applying to universities in Scotland, then your young person could be asked to specialise for their four-year degree from the beginning of year one.

At the time of writing in 2024, Duncan of Jordanstone College of Art and Design in Dundee (DJCAD) and Gray's School of Art (Robert Gordon University) in Aberdeen still have a general first year, like a Foundation Diploma course. Students are then asked to specialise from year 2.

It is not guaranteed that your young person will progress into their first choice in their second year. Therefore, hard work to pass the first year and a selection process often takes place to ensure that the students are suitably matched for the subject that they wish to proceed on to.

Please see the individual institutions websites for details of applying from a Foundation Diploma course to a four-year degree course in Scotland.

HNC/D Courses

Your young person may be in a position where they haven't been successful in applying for a degree programme. And yet, they don't wish to do a Foundation Diploma course because they know which subject they wish to specialise in.

Or maybe they just know which subject they wish to specialise in, however they're not qualified for the degree course.

This could be an ideal opportunity to apply for a Higher National Diploma (HND) or a Higher National Certificate (HNC).

An HND is a 2-year specialised course, after the first year you are awarded your HNC. Some students see this as a stepping stone to a degree, and it can allow you to enter the second or third year of a degree programme for example. Some students complete the first year of the HND which will award them the HNC, and then apply for university after the HNC, which is what I would recommend.

Historically HNC/D courses were more vocational and had strong links with industry. It was rare to find an HNC/D in Fine Art as we discussed in Chapter 2, it's more often that a Fine Art course would lead to self-employment as an artist. However, there are courses in the Fine Art and Contemporary Art Practice areas at further education colleges now at HNC/D level.

If applying to a HNC/D course the application is also made direct to the college as with Foundation Diploma courses.

The highest-level course that your young person may be considering applying to from school will be a degree course.

Your young person will make their application to UCAS, which acts as a central body and forwards their application to the institutions on their behalf.

At the time of writing in 2024, applicants are allowed five choices. You may add to this later in the process with UCAS Extra if you're not holding any offers or none that you wish to accept.

Many parents and students don't realise the full extent of the process required for an art and design submission to university or art school – or the timescale involved.

I'll clarify that with you in this Chapter here, I'm basing it on the UCAS system here in the UK and is subject to change.

Other College Courses for 16 Up

Sometimes there are students who wish to leave school after their GCSEs or National 5 exams, who perhaps don't feel school is the best place for them.

There are several BTEC courses and National Certificate courses (in Scotland) that cover a broad introduction to art and design.

These will take your young person on a journey towards higher level courses, such as the Foundation Diploma course or HNC/D courses if they wish.

Similar to the other courses at further education colleges, the application is made direct to the college.

At this stage you don't necessarily need to choose one course over another. If your young person is qualified (or will be after their current exams) they can, if they wish, apply to university and have a backup plan of a Foundation Diploma and/or HNC/D. Because the universities recruit through UCAS and the further college directly to the college, both are an option.

However, it's important to ensure your young person knows the course's accreditation level and that it doesn't repeat their previous art and design experience, as this can lead to a lack of motivation and inspiration.

If your young person is considering a course at BTEC or NC then they will be qualified at that level, not any higher.

I would recommend to all students to have a back-up plan, however good they consider their chances to be.

Application Deadlines

Let's start at the end – like any artist, we're here to break the rules!

Your young person does need to be aware that the dates when they need to apply to courses at university vs further education college are different.

There are set deadlines for UCAS for university applications, and it can vary depending on the university. I would recommend checking UCAS to confirm which application dates are relevant to your application.

In my experience some schools like to have their students complete and submit their applications early when other subject applications are required in October.

However, I wouldn't advise this as it can significantly reduce the time that a student has to work on their artwork that is needed for the content of the portfolio. We go into this much deeper in the coming Chapters.

A happy medium is required, and this needs planning and a discussion between your young person and their teachers/guidance, as soon as they know they wish to apply for art and design at university.

Once the UCAS application is submitted, your young person will hear from the institutions with an invitation to submit examples of their artwork in the form of a portfolio.

Please beware of submitting the UCAS application early, in October or November for example. If your young person does this, they could be asked to submit their portfolio very soon after this. Ideally, they will want as long as possible to work on their portfolio before they are called to submit it.

For those applying in the rest of the UK (not including Scotland), once the UCAS application is submitted, the call to submit your portfolio could be within 2 weeks.

I have heard from school art teachers last year that some of their students have been called (on an automated email from the institutions) to submit their portfolios over the Christmas holidays. This can be problematic if a UCAS application is submitted at the end of term, just before the Christmas holidays. Don't get caught out here, as there are only a few teachers I imagine would be happy to help on Christmas Day, which did happen!

If you're applying for courses in Scotland, their dates are set for submitting your portfolio. For example, at the time of writing in 2024, submission dates for the Edinburgh College of Art (University of Edinburgh) and Glasgow School of Art are in early February.

These dates apply to everyone, whatever date you've submitted your UCAS application (International students usually have longer to submit, please consult the individual institution). DJCAD and Gray's School of Art are slightly later but dates are always made public and are confirmed on their websites.

The closing date for non-university applications, for further education courses (Foundation, HNC/D and BTEC or NC courses) varies from college to college; however, it's usually around March onwards. Please do check out the individual institution's website for all details of the entry requirements, including grades from school and portfolio procedures.

Timelines and When to Get Started

Given that the UCAS is the first deadline, it's my advice to start researching the universities or further education college courses (if your young person is considering) as soon as possible.

Getting started at the beginning of the academic year (August/September) with the college and university research allows your young person around 20 weeks to really focus their mind on which courses and subjects they wish to apply to.

This then gives the very best opportunity for the creation of the artwork that they can produce in the time before January to be strong and relevant for the courses they've chosen.

And it does take this long – if they are aiming for any of the country's more competitive courses where there may only be 13-18 places available to students worldwide, please don't underestimate the commitment and time required.

Every December, I receive enquiries from students who realise they haven't given enough thought to their portfolios and meeting deadlines, and they start to panic that it's too late.

And when is too late?

I'd say December is starting too late. And January is definitely too late!

Too late to start pulling together artwork that has no thread demonstrating a clear creative process.

Also, too late to be seeking assistance from tutors like myself who will be careering towards the deadlines of the new year with the students they've been supporting since September.

The stress that this causes both students, parents and tutors just isn't worth it.

When individuals are stressed, they are least likely to be able to be creative. Creativity is really hampered by time. There are the odd few people who really work well under fierce deadlines, but most find it too overwhelming.

My recommendation is to start with a focused plan at the start of the academic year that your young person is applying. So if they are heading for the UCAS January deadlines, to start the previous August/September. I'd also advise not just following the school curriculum but creating work outside of school as we'll go into more in Chapter 6 on Content.

At this early stage, it's also prudent for your young person to ask their teachers what and how much support they give to students applying to university/art school. It's perhaps assumed that this is part of the A level or Advanced Higher course. However, in my experience, it varies greatly from school to school, teacher to teacher.

If your young person's teachers don't support compiling an application, including the portfolio, with them, then engaging someone experienced to support you is essential.

There is a distinct difference between pulling together a selection of your best work and planning a portfolio for success at some of the country's most competitive courses.

Ten days is not enough if you've left it that late. Please don't let your young person do this to you!

Your Tasks

Now that your young person knows where they are and what they will be qualified to study, they can begin to do online research into which courses they feel drawn to.

I'd advise at this stage to look out for college and university Open Days and for them to book for attendance. The best and only way to really find out if a university or college and a particular course is right for your young person is to visit each that they are considering.

If your young person is considering moving away from home, this gives them a real feeling for the actual city, as three or four years is a considerable amount of time to spend there if it's not right.

And not all courses across the country are the same.

It's also wise to look at the course specifications which will be on the universities' and colleges' websites. This will give you both a thorough understanding of the course content, modules, weighting of any written units and elective elements that may allow cross-disciplinary learning in other areas of the university.

"Creativity is allowing yourself to make mistakes, art is knowing which ones to keep."

Scott Adams, Author and Cartoonist

5

What Mindset Should You Adopt?

Dealing with Failure
Curiosity, Courage and Clarity
Resilience
Daring to Be Different vs. Trying to Fit In
Assumptions That Need to Be Challenged
Unlearning and Play

5

What Mindset Should You Adopt?

This Chapter is a biggie.

We touched upon some mindset shifts required in Chapter 3 on creativity. We will go deeper in this Chapter, as it really is the crux of what makes the contents of your young person's portfolio "good enough" or not.

Your young person's mindset is THE most important thing that they can work on, and that will catapult them from struggling with lack of awareness and overwhelm to flying and loving it!

The most important thing to work on is not mastering techniques to be better and better, or getting higher and higher grades at school, aiming for an A*.

Unfortunately, this mindset that is required is quite different in my view, to what is going on currently in schools. Yes, your young person needs to ensure that they are meeting the academic grades that are required but read on for what is AS important.

In Chapter 3 we discussed what creativity is, and what the problems surrounding it are: such as "testing culture" and how that impacts creativity. Hopefully, you have watched the Cindy Foley TED talk, because then you'll have a greater understanding of this now.

If your young person is going to thrive in the creative industries, they will be so much better equipped if they can embrace the mindsets below.

As a byproduct of mastering the mindsets below, the transferable and employability skills that we spoke about in Chapter 2 will automatically be bolstered. They *will* thrive into their degree and beyond.

Mastering these mindsets now will save a LOT of work during a degree. They will be able to hit the ground running and will give your young person confidence that just doesn't happen without this focus on intention.

The mindsets they need to master are as follows:

- Dealing with failure
- Resilience
- Curiosity and courage
- Daring to be different vs. fitting in
- Expectation
- Unlearning and play

Dealing with Failure

Failure for ourselves is something that makes us feel sad, frustrated and not worthy.

As we often speak and do from experience, it's even more difficult to see our kids fail - because ultimately we can't do the work for them or change the reality.

Personally, I'll do (almost!) anything to ensure that our daughter, who's now sitting her first exams this year, does not fail. How about you? And I know full well it's not good for her to never fail, but it's still painful to watch!

I'm not talking about letting your young person fail to get into art college. Although having said that, sometimes that IS a good thing, again, speaking from experience!

But the very act of failing builds the next mindset in the list that creatives really NEED to be: resilient.

I'm talking about failure in terms of your young person allowing themselves to fail at making "good" art.

Failure to fulfil the design brief adequately.

Failing to master a certain artistic process/technique.

Failing to make a masterpiece every time they put pen/pencil/paint to paper.

Failing to make every page in their sketchbook amazing.

Failure is a part of the creative process, and if your young person is ever to succeed, failure is no doubt partly responsible for it.

Ultimately, they need to get comfortable with failure.

I discussed my experience with perfectionism in Chapter 3, and it's one of the main reasons why many students don't get the offers that they are hoping for.

This scenario happened to Anna, who worked painfully slowly at school, not producing enough, and focusing on realism alone. It was partly for this reason that she failed to get the offer she wanted straight out of school.

She found it very difficult to challenge this idea of perfectionism because the school system had rewarded her for it, with a grade A!

Her dad Tony noticed this and knew that with Anna working so slowly and meticulously, the likelihood of her having enough work would be slim. My advice of quantity to ACHIEVE quality was really harnessed when we worked together on her portfolio. She became much more carefree, which resulted in more spontaneous works being produced, and mountains of the stuff! When you've produced lots of work – what happens, according to Walt Stanchfield?

Yes, I am referring to this quote again: "We all have 10,000 bad drawings in us. The sooner we get them out the better." Then the good ones get produced – and those are what we want for their portfolio.

And how can they learn to get comfortable with failure? We'll cover that in the upcoming section on unlearning and play.

Curiosity, Courage and Clarity

I'm grouping these together as they form my "3 Cs approach".

Two of the main attributes that will bring strength to your young person's application, portfolio and outlook on creative life are that of curiosity and courage.

When we talk about courage, we often think we need confidence first. However, my experience with students shows that if they can sit with discomfort in their artwork – feeling scared, out of their comfort zone, and unsure of the results – confidence will follow. We earn confidence by doing things that scare us, to a degree.

This means, yes you've got it, we have to do things *without* confidence sometimes, this takes courage.

So now, can you see why I encourage your young person to start early with their art and design application and portfolio? Because unless they have plenty of time, they don't have *time* to fail or to do things that scare them. As a result, they don't build the confidence they need to do something more exciting than what they know they're good at and what the curriculum defines.

Curiosity can be a double-edged sword. We have so much access to so much information in the digital world, that we can spend our whole lives being curious about *everything*!

However, if you were to compare a young person who isn't curious about *anything* and a person who is curious about *everything*, my judgement is that the latter would be preferential and demonstrate a highly creative individual.

Therefore, when I discuss curiosity, I mean being curious on a number of levels.

Firstly, being curious about the world and what is happening in the world; being curious about people; and being curious about themselves and what makes them tick.

If a student isn't curious, they will have little to contribute in terms of ideas and concepts in their art. Without curiosity about their materials and techniques, their portfolio will remain narrow, showcasing only what they feel they have "mastered".

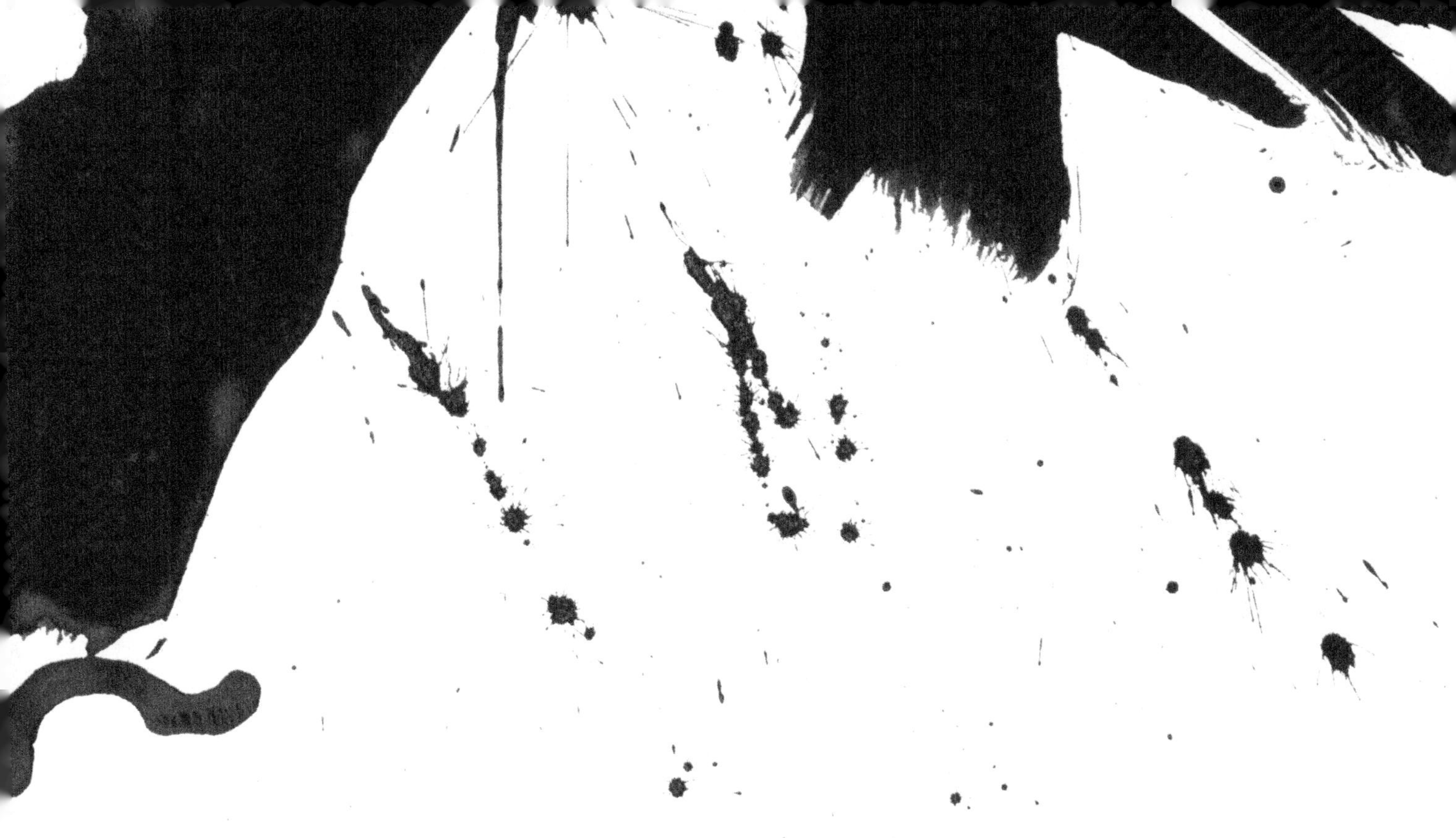

"If you're not prepared to be wrong, you'll never come up with anything original."

Sir Ken Robinson, Author and Orator

A strong portfolio is intrinsically linked to curiosity.

What can your young person do to get more curious about the world and themselves?

What can your young person do to build curiosity of art materials, art processes and their day-to-day art practice?

The courage and curiosity that is needed when adopting a "What would happen if –?" approach should not be underestimated.

When I taught printmaking at Edinburgh College of Art, it was very much technique and process-based. Students would often ask me what would happen if they did a certain thing to their artwork.

So, for example, what would happen if they tried using watercolour underneath printing from a wood block? In my early teaching days, I often launched into explaining, trying to be helpful, what would happen and how it may not be a good idea if that's what I genuinely thought.

However, having had many years of experience teaching students in all areas of art and design at Edinburgh College of Art and further education colleges, I began to respond with "Why don't you try it and see what happens?"

This was significantly more beneficial for the student because it gave them evidence of what would happen. This approach would provide content for their sketchbook (the creative process), and it would provide experiential learning, which far surpasses passive learning in terms of embedding knowledge. And let's not forget, it also provides fun and joy in the unexpected, a win-win!

Additionally, as I didn't really know what they were aiming to achieve with their artwork (maybe they didn't either), we were on a learning journey together. And when unexpected things happen, sometimes these are the most interesting and exciting times.

You might be asking, where the heck does clarity fit into all this?

By going through this process of being curious, with courage, then clarity starts to appear. By trying new things, deciding what your young person enjoys, what works, what does not, what is important to them, this paves the way for greater clarity over where they are going and how they are going to get there.

Cue: Resilience!

Resilience

As parents, we know that life isn't always easy – it's not meant to be, I guess. I recall during my younger years, believing that once I resolved any challenges or unexpected circumstances, life would become easy and "perfect".

But of course, problems come and go, and we can't always solve them. No sooner than one is solved, others crop up here and there – life is a rich tapestry like that.

However, much of the creative process is about solving problems. And I believe that being able to solve these kinds of small-scale creative problems gives us the skills to solve larger, more complex life problems.

Problem-solving builds resilience – in your young person's creativity as well as in their life in the broader context.

The more resilient we can be to small adversities in life, the better we get at flexing those muscles. So, when there is a BIG thing to flex against, these muscles are strong, and we can cope.

In this section, I want to touch upon the subject of mental health. I have a huge interest in this, as all parents do, as we're seeing an exponential rise in mental health issues in our young people.

I don't think that mental health problems are isolated to those creatives. We're seeing it popping up here, there and everywhere, and it's my belief that lifestyle is a huge factor.

However, I do believe that creative souls perhaps are more sensitive, they possibly question aspects of life more, maybe over-thinking due to curiosity (oh yes, there's downsides to being curious I guess too!).

But these character traits are also our superpowers. Our secret sauce. And that's what I love to nurture and support.

It can be painful to watch your young person struggle in this way.

But in recent years, I've been collating my own library of resources to help bring more self-awareness to young people to enable them to live richer, fuller, creative lives.

This section on resilience is vast and I could write forever. An aspect touched upon in the above ideas, which I encourage you and your young person to explore further together, is the concept of comfort versus discomfort.

It's true of life and it's true in creativity.

We've never had a time in society where we have more luxury, physical comfort, heating in homes and cars, and no need to move to order food, we go from sitting at home to sitting in our cars, to sitting at work/school to sitting in the evening relaxing. Yet we're challenged significantly by mental health issues that give us deep and uncontrollable discomfort.

By challenging our bodies AND minds more in supported ways to fully experience more *dis*comfort, we can build resilience in our lives.

I think this powerful quote by David Bowie sums it up perfectly:

> **"If you feel safe in the area you are working in, then you are not working in the right area. Always go a little further into the water than you think you feel you're capable of being in. Go a little bit out of your depth. Then, when you don't feel that your feet are quite touching the bottom, you're just about in the right place to do something exciting."**

(Incidentally, I don't think he's talking about swimming!)

Daring to be Different vs. Trying to Fit In

I remember it well: I didn't want to be different.

I wanted to fit in, wear the right stuff, not look out of place. I think this is common with teenagers, and it's probably not until an individual is a little older that they feel the courage and confidence to express themselves more individually, to really be who they are or aspire to be.

I often hear from students that they're going to study a certain subject in their art "because that's what everyone else is doing" or "because a pupil last year did this topic and they got a high grade".

I understand where this is coming from; however, it's a valid reason not to work on that specific subject if they aim to showcase their uniqueness and different ideas from others.

Doing what others have done before will cement in the assessors' minds that it's just another school application, someone who is going through the motions and jumping through the curriculum hoops.

University art and design applications reward students who are different, who think differently and who are prepared to go out on a limb to be noticed - risking taking if you like.

My advice for your young person is to think about what makes them different, embrace their "weird" and exploit it as much as possible in their portfolio.

The part of my tutoring and mentoring that I find most enjoyable is learning about the individual students, how they view the world, what makes them different and what makes them tick, and then helping them to exploit that through their creative work.

And this is exactly what Claudia embraced in her portfolio, which we discussed in Chapter 1.

Her mind was buzzing with the many interests that she had. And most were BIG ideas. By that I mean they had many facets that she hadn't drilled down into smaller parts of the whole.

That aside, they were interests that others would also have - space, the universe etc. But one thing she spoke about that influenced her day-to-day life greatly was her experiences of orthodontic care and her resulting Obsessive Compulsive Disorder (OCD) about her teeth.

Yes, many of us have orthodontic experiences too, me included. However her experience and her behaviours, thoughts and offering a glimpse into this, is what super-powered her portfolio. She explored using the tools and materials that she cared for her teeth (brushes, mouthwash, straws that she drank with) to make art with and about.

Your young person might think they have nothing that makes them very different to the next person, but if they look hard enough, they really can find more than they think. Claudia used her curiosity and courage about herself to gain clarity. Claudia went on to study at DJCAD and is, at the time of writing, a 3D animator at Paper Snake.

Using this simple yet unique example, what unusual interests, habits, or observations in life does your young person have that others might not notice?

By using this "different-ness" in their work, communicating this in some way, it will turn heads on the selection panel, be memorable, and ultimately elevate their ranking against portfolios that are pretty vanilla.

Assumptions that Need to be Challenged

I want to address common assumptions about art and design education post school, especially regarding parental expectations, challenging these often-held beliefs.

It's important to be realistic about your and your young person's expectations based on these assumptions, as well as the information and misinformation out there.

Let's kick it off with:

The assumption that a student is heading for a grade A at high school, so they are bound to be offered a place on their chosen course.
This isn't always true and should not be an assumption that is relied upon for reasons we've discussed earlier in this Chapter.

The assumption that a student is applying for a very competitive course, some have only places for 13 students, so they'll never be offered a place when there's so much competition.
Yes, competition is high in many of the creative industries' courses. Mindset needs to be strong, resilience high, and having the support to believe in your dreams and make them a reality, it is achievable. I always say to students that someone has to get those 13 places, so it might as well be you.

An expectation that is loaded on them from parents and/or teachers.
This can be a tough one. My only guidance here is that your young person really has to want it from *their* heart. If they are applying for university from a sense of outside pressure or to please others, then it's unlikely to be a strong enough reason. It will show in the portfolio, lacking that individuality and passion that's needed in the overall application. Sometimes a student just isn't ready to make big decisions like applying to university from school. In Scotland, many students leaving school will be only 17 and occasionally a little extra time either at college or working can make a huge difference to motivation, confidence and ultimately success.

There is also an assumption that if they have additional support needs or if there's disruption to their studies, it puts them at a disadvantage and that some courses and universities will be out of their reach.

These thoughts need some attention based on the individual and the institution. There are guidelines in each university's application process that can assist to level the playing field and take into account your young person's individual situation. The cookie cutter approach as we know doesn't always work, and some students need one-to-one support with their application and creative work. Seek this information out early on in your research by contacting admissions at the university or college that your young person has an interest in. Ask specific questions about their exact position to find out what support they offer for students with more complex applications.

Unlearning and Play

When we go through the school system, we start in primary school being pretty free and easy about what we create. Remember our daughter's experience with the scribbles – and how she felt as a result?

If by embracing some of the mindset in this Chapter, your young person can allow themselves to play and unlearn some of the "rules" that don't necessarily serve them well (other than to pass in the school system), they will be making strong progress.

I love this quote by artist Christine Evans:

> **"I'm not painting, I'm practising, I'm practising being thoughtless and uncritical and spontaneous. I'm not thinking, just putting marks down, putting marks down, putting some more marks down and then I'm just sitting back and going 'hmmm what do I like here?"**

Next time your young person is starting a piece of artwork or project, ask them to set a timer on their phone, two minutes for example. See what they can do (in a sketchbook would be ideal, but paper is fine) within this timeframe.

Ask them to choose three new materials that they're not used to working with *and* set their timer for two minutes. See what they can achieve.

Then sit back, reflect and ask, what do I like here? What's making me happy here? What do I dislike? And the critical question to follow all of these initial questions is "Why?" If you dislike something, why do you dislike it? This can go a long way to helping with the creative process and building on that inquisitive, curious nature.

And in response to these questions - "Nothing" is not an option!

If they can note these answers down, this will start a little bank of experiments and fun that they can learn from, to apply in a more deliberate way next time. It also establishes the habit of using a sketchbook and engaging in reflection and justification, which are evaluated in the portfolio process discussed in Chapter 6 on Content.

Your Tasks

- What can your young person do to get more curious about the world and themselves?

They can begin by being a little more self-aware, and start to notice what their character traits are, their interests, their quirks etc. that make them who they are and different to the next person. Sometimes it's easier done with others as we don't always see this ourselves, so how can you help them?

- What can your young person do to build curiosity about art materials, art processes and their day-to-day art practice?

As I mentioned previously, ask them to choose three new materials that they're not used to working with *and* set their timer for two minutes and see what they can achieve in that time and reflect on this with those reflection questions.

Begin an art session by adopting the following question "What would happen if –?" This promotes courage and curiosity that is needed in the creative process, that should not be underestimated.

"Research is to see what everybody else has seen, and to think what nobody else has thought."

Albert Szent-Gyorgyi, Hungarian Biochemist,
Nobel Prize for Medicine

6 What Content Will You Use for Applications?

What Content Will You Use for Applications?

There are multiple pieces of evidence that your young person needs to provide to demonstrate their creativity and suitability for any particular course.

It's not quite so straightforward as some other subjects - applying to university, getting your grades and then receiving an offer or a conditional offer. Yes, the UCAS application, statement, exam grades are all important, and these qualify you even to be considered for art and design courses at university.

However, once qualified, your young person's portfolio, possibly a set task, a further written statement specific to each institution, and an interview will be the critical factors in receiving an offer.

This requires a significant investment of time and it's advisable to get started early!

Having said this, it can be enjoyable and hopefully *will* be enjoyable for your young person.

However, if your young person isn't fully aware of what is required from the outset, it can be quite overwhelming when this comes in addition to mock and preliminary exams that take place at a similar time.

By knowing what they will experience early on, you can both manage your expectations and stress levels.

It is very dependent on the university as to exactly which elements of the contents of this Chapter will be asked for.

I've found with students that when it's a task that's managed together with parent and young person, the burden, the planning, and the organisation needed becomes much easier to handle for everyone. From my experience, many creative students are dyslexic, which can hinder their ability to organise and manage this part of the application. Any help you can provide is truly invaluable.

The Written Statement and Application

The first part of the application is the online written application that, if applying to universities, will go through the central body UCAS (which we discussed in Chapter 4).

If applying for further education courses - a BTEC, NC, foundation course or HNC/D for example, then the application will be made direct to the college.

Additionally, some universities ask for a further statement when the student submits the portfolio – we'll come to that.

The personal statement is your young person's first chance to tell the universities and colleges why they should be selected – it might be their last!

Not many universities make a preliminary selection based on the UCAS application alone (composed of your exam results and personal statement). However, some do. So your young person can treat it as a "first hurdle" so to speak, to give it the attention it needs.

When I worked at Edinburgh College of Art, the personal statement really came into its own if we had two students who were scoring very similar in their exam results and creative ability. It was seen as a way to make the final selections on who had the edge over other students.

So the personal statement does matter - it can be the difference between being offered a place or not.

Your young person needs to demonstrate their enthusiasm and commitment to the subject specialism that they are applying to, and above all, ensure that they stand out from the crowd – which they do, right?

In my experience, advice from guidance at schools is to approach the personal statement in a similar way to other academic subjects. Therefore, including achievements, hobbies, prefect duties, Duke of Edinburgh Award, extra curricular activities, etc. are usually encouraged.

My advice, though, is to keep this for one paragraph towards the end.
The majority of your young person's statement needs to be about their experience with art, their challenges, reflections and interests in the art and design world.

I advise them not to write anything that they are not confident to talk about at an interview.

Because they're called "personal statements", students often think, "Hmmm…'personal'…I'll talk about me then". But please proceed with caution. To really get noticed, encourage your young person not to just talk about themselves, but to start communicating with the college or university they are applying for – talk about their subject of art or design in relation to your young person's *experience* of it.

I've read a lot of personal statements and many first drafts that start with something similar to "from an early age I have loved art/drawing/painting etc." and how "I'm devoted to study, am motivated, organised, and passionate" etc. This is very clichéd - if you're applying to a university/art college, they will expect all that as a given.

Most people write their personal statement in an essay style, starting off with the course and why they want to do it, how they are suited to it, what they want to gain from studying it, then talking about their relevant work experience and skills, finishing off with extracurricular activities – but as a creative person, your young person can choose any style that works for them.

The most important advice I can give is to follow closely the guidance given from UCAS or the individual universities if applying outside of UCAS, as guidelines can and do change. There may be a set of questions that are given as guidance to form your statement. It's crucial that your young person demonstrates their suitability for the course within the scope of the question criteria.

The Reference

Your young person will need to ask someone to be their referee for their application.

The referee should be someone who knows your young person academically and can share information relevant to the courses they're applying for, along with any predicted grades for qualifications they're currently studying.

It's important that this person knows your young person and their artwork, and can speak in the context of the creative specialism that they're applying for. This will often be an art teacher at school or a college tutor.

It's not advisable to ask a work employer if your young person is currently in work, as they won't have the specialist knowledge, nor would they be able to say how suitable your young person is for an art and design course. In this scenario, I would advise that they return to school to ask if their former art teacher is happy to be the referee.

Alternatively, if they've not been in education for some time, consider someone who can comment on their artwork and their ability to study the course that they're applying for. Some universities may consider an employment reference; however, it's best to clarify this with the institutions that you're applying to.

A Portfolio of Work

Clarity around what a portfolio IS, is important. It is something that is often assumed that we know.

Ultimately, it's quite simple – but not easy. There is so much information out there about what a portfolio is, it's rather overwhelming. One parent once referred to it as "My swim through the Google information ocean..." He admitted he and his daughter had spent so long searching for information about what a portfolio is, that the more they discovered, the more confused they became.

At a basic level, a portfolio is a collection of artworks that your young person feels proud of, that shows their interests in the world and their skills in creativity. Note that I say skills in *creativity*, not artistic skills, please check and revisit Chapter 3 on Creativity.

The most important aspect of a portfolio is that it is a personal response by your young person, not a cookie cutter approach based on school projects.

One of the biggest mistakes that students can make is to limit the understanding of "work that they're most pleased with" to only final pieces. By showing only their final pieces, universities will see only a fraction of what they are asking to see.

Your young person could then score low in the assessment criteria that awards marks for showing ideas, rough sketches, how ideas have been developed and which artists and designers have been influential.

There also needs to be some cohesion of thought and projects that show the full creative or design process – not a collection of random pieces that are disconnected.

To understand deeper why this is important, you can download the free PDF in the resources area at www.portfolio-oomph.com/creativecareers on "How to avoid the top 10 mistakes holding you back from getting into art school".

A strong portfolio is likely to include work from school if indeed your young person is at school. And by this, I mean recent schoolwork - so A level work, Higher and Advanced Higher work. Going back beyond this, to GCSE and National 5 qualification, is considered old work and should not be used (unless applying for college directly after GCSE/National 5).

In my view, seeing work in a portfolio that is more than one or two years old shows poor selection. It also shows that a student doesn't have enough current work that demonstrates the consistent commitment to art and design that studying at a higher level demands.

However, if they're applying to a university level course, the portfolio should also include work that has been done outside of school.

When I worked on the portfolio selection interview process at Edinburgh College of Art (University of Edinburgh), we would assess and interview candidates from the same school on the same days. This enabled us to see the projects that were recurrent across several portfolios. We could see which students had a greater skill level, which ones went over and beyond what the teacher had asked in projects at school, and which had attended extra classes or worked on self-initiated projects.

If possible, your young person should link the work done in any extra classes to a theme or interest they have of their own. This is preferable to a collection of random pieces of work that purely demonstrate the learning of an art or design technique that doesn't have a purpose beyond this.

They may wish to attend life drawing workshops. These are plentiful in most cities and towns, at weekends or an evening class. Life drawing *isn't* essential however it is helpful for certain courses where understanding the figure is important. For example, it may be useful in fashion design – being able to draw clothing on a figure, perhaps animation where most characters within animations require reference to proportion and movement in relation to the figure. The fine art areas also are interested in life drawing; though it's not essential.

The expectation for further education courses isn't so much on work done outside of school. But anything that your young person can do that shows commitment above and beyond the standard school curriculum will increase their chances of acceptance.

Subject Specialisms

Your young person will be asked to choose to apply from many areas of art and design – painting, graphic design, illustration, textiles, performance costume, interior design, architecture, photography, jewellery, product design, fashion design, sculpture and others.

Although your young person's work will most likely include general drawing and technique-based work, it is important for them to show how their interests are related to the subject specialism they're applying for.

For example, a portfolio in application for jewellery should not predominantly be work that is drawing and painting. Likewise, a student applying for photography should really have predominantly photography in their portfolio.

This is not to say that your young person needs to have professionalism in jewellery skills. But demonstrating an understanding of three-dimensional forms, strong making skills and 3D visualisation within the portfolio should be evident.

Take another example such as textile design, where a student would be expected to have a good understanding of colour and combinations, pattern, repetition and some kind of construction with textiles and other materials.

Remember the universities aren't looking for the finished item, as in they're not looking for a professional artist or designer. They're looking to assess your young person's potential to develop into the area that they're applying for. So, consider the skills that would be used in the area that they're applying for and then demonstrate these within their portfolio.

Another way to demonstrate suitability for a specialist subject is by incorporating influential artists and designers from that area into their creative process.

But if they don't address the specific area that they are applying for in the portfolio, UCAS statement and/or sketchbooks, their portfolio will be marked lower and it may cost them their place to someone who can better demonstrate their commitment to the subject specialism.

It might come as a surprise to you that some universities don't currently require a portfolio for some subjects. For example, the University of Edinburgh (ECA) doesn't, at the time of writing, ask for a portfolio at all for architecture. However, University College London's (UCL) Bartlett School of Architecture has a very rigorous, multi-facetted selection process, including a set task/home assignment in addition to the portfolio.

But in the main, a portfolio is required, so it is imperative from the outset that you and your young person find out what is required to help this process run as smoothly as possible.

The Portfolio Folder

In the good old days when we used to travel around the country with our portfolio to interview, it was contained in an A1 or A2 size folder. However, these days not many universities interview students in person, so a digital portfolio is required – which I will also explain.

"Learn the rules like a pro, so you can break them like an artist."

Pablo Picasso, Artist

It is still good practice for your young person to have a portfolio folder that contains their work during creation, to protect the work and keep it flat. My advice would be to buy an A1 portfolio, the best that you can afford.

The Creative Process

I mentioned earlier that one of the most common mistakes that students make is thinking that only the final pieces of work form the portfolio. And in Chapter 3 on Creativity, we explored what the problem is with our understanding of what creativity means. Here I aim to delve a little more into how the notion of creativity fits into the portfolio.

Part of a strong portfolio should show the process and some of the developmental pieces that went before the final pieces were made. This could be some of the experiments, sketches, testing of materials and techniques – even the things that didn't work out.

Often there is the misunderstanding that the process means the documenting of the cumulative incremental stages of creating one final piece of work – a day by day record if you like. However, this isn't what is meant by how a piece has been developed.

And this process can take place in the sketchbook or on paper – some of this might even be mounted (if your young person is taking their portfolio and attending a face-to-face interview) and presented as key elements of the process. This should certainly be presented as a part of a digital portfolio.

There are two drawbacks to not doing the creative process/development work, also by not showing it.

If one doesn't do it then the final pieces will be weak. Generally, when we've had an idea and then just make it, draw it, it's often not that strong. Therefore, final pieces will be weak AND there won't be any developmental work to show. This results in two areas of the portfolio being weak.

If one does engage in the creative process but doesn't show it in the portfolio submission, then the final outcomes may well be strong. However the development stages that are also assessed will score low. This makes an overall lower score, and results in potentially not being accepted on course.

Drawing should be highly evident in sketchbooks AND in the portfolio as this is the primary means of putting ideas down on paper so that others can see what they're imagining.

Drawing demonstrates a basic understanding of forms, tone, and structure and communicates to the viewer what your young person's ideas are. Or if working in the design areas, it communicates to a potential client what the ideas are so a dialogue can take place to refine the ideas to completion.

This is not only a good way for your young person to work through ideas, but it is the only way any tutor or teacher can really help them with the development of their ideas. Tutors cannot help anyone if their ideas are stuck inside their head; your young person can perhaps see them clearly, but we can't!

Whether studying for fashion design, sculpture, animation or jewellery, drawing will be central to a strong portfolio and sketchbooks – which we'll cover in the next section of this Chapter.

I suggest that a range of materials and techniques should also be evident. But it doesn't have to be the primary or sole focus.

And please be mindful of how we discussed in Chapter 3, about the scope of what drawing can be. If your young person hasn't already looked at my Pinterest board full of exciting ways to approach drawing, now would be the perfect time to do so. You can find a link to my Pinterest drawing board in the resources area at www.portfolio-oomph.com/creativecareers.

If your young person is attending an in-person interview with their portfolio, then it's essential that they pay attention to the presentation of the work by mounting it. I would advise mounting on white card/heavy duty paper.

In addition to work that is mounted – the portfolio should also contain sketchbooks showing the creative or design process.

Sketchbooks

A critical part of your portfolio that frequently doesn't get covered at school is working in sketchbooks. If it is covered, my experience is that it is often pieces of work carefully stuck in with a lot of time being spent on decorating it to look pretty. This isn't going to get you any more marks, sadly.

Students find this the most challenging aspect of a portfolio because it's where they would gather and record the process that they're going through whilst creating their artworks.

To reiterate, a sketchbook shouldn't be a curated collection of successful pieces of artwork that have been stuck in.

Ideally, it needs to be a workbook that your young person works straight into, and includes experiments, mistakes and documentation of their process. This should include annotations about their thoughts and decision-making, and provide to the viewer some insight into how you're exploring your subject or idea.

You can find a link to some beautiful examples on my Pinterest sketchbook board in the resources area at www.portfolio-oomph.com/creativecareers.

Experimentation

Sketchbooks are a place to try things out, experiment and above all, to have some fun with. Treating every page as a masterpiece will achieve nothing, and each page will be a trial to even get started.

The sketchbook is a tool to record the process of ideas through to the final piece. If bad ideas/works are being removed, this hides the selection and judgement process that has taken place to get to some great final pieces. And ultimately, this is a part of the university selection criteria.

The universities will want to see evidence of your decision making and selection processes. Difficult as it may be for them, do encourage your young person not to rip pages out.

Writing Thoughts and Others

Your young person can write down in their sketchbooks thoughts, textures, sounds, conversations, photos, objects, samples of stitching/ fabrics/mixed media pieces, and other things that they find of interest. Like a diary – use it as a thinking space, but with visuals and words.

The Process

This illustration shows the four stages of the creative process that your young person should be aiming to demonstrate in their portfolio.

1

RESEARCH/VISUAL ENQUIRY

Show through images that you are engaged in research/ visual enquiry of your subject/concept of some kind.

2

DEVELOPMENT WORK

Documentation of the journey you have taken from idea/ concept to finished piece.

3

CONTEXTUAL AWARENESS

Visual evidence of artists/designers that you align yourself with and why you are interested in them. Demonstrate basic research of the subject area that you are interested in.

CRITICAL JUDGEMENT, SELECTION AND RESOLVED WORK

Now that you have gone from the idea/concept to the finished piece, show the choices that you have made along the way; how can you demonstrate this?

The first three of these stages can be worked on in their sketchbook.

1. Research/Visual Enquiry

Research (which often results in ideas) is vital to any creative process, and it *is* a process. After all, how are we to get inspired if we don't engage in research? Ideas don't often drop out of the sky onto our lap, or at least they don't for me or anyone else I know. I have trouble getting this through to students, day in and day out, and many refuse to accept this. The problem is, they're still waiting for the ideas to drop, while many others get the places at university before them!

Research is the initial exploration, and importantly recording of ideas, things, places, objects and notions. The collection of these is the start of the creative process. It should be a broad-ranging and in-depth, experimental, investigative, personal process that leads your young person to know more about their subject or project brief. It will provide a creative direction and purpose to their efforts.

I always say to students that if they are struggling with ideas or if their ideas are just dull, then they have not done enough research. This is true for design and fine art areas.

There are two types of research:

Primary research pertains to things that your young person has discovered, collected or recorded first hand. Objects that they have drawn from, photographed, taken a rubbing from, mono-printed from, etc. that we often engage with in a much more meaningful relationship as our other senses have been involved. That is to say, we've touched it, smelt it, and had memories of using it or being in that particular place.

Secondary research, however, pertains to findings that other people have made, for instance on the internet, in books or magazines, journals etc. This kind of research can be good, as it allows us to read, hear, and watch things that we don't have access to and inspire us in other ways. Secondary research is no less important than primary research, but I would emphasise that having only secondary research as the starting point is not a good idea. It's beneficial to have a good mixture of both, otherwise, your young person will not have the opportunity to show their drawing skills from life.

Research should be fun, exploratory, exciting and more importantly, USEFUL.

2. Development Work

As your young person engages with the physical or material world, how are they exploring *how* these things work; *how* do they understand them?

There are a few ways that your young person might choose to develop their work and I will make a round-up of the ways that I find useful in developing and exploring my ideas.

Layering, repeating, enlarging/reducing, abstracting, material-based exploration, collage and texture. There are more ways to develop work, and it's up to your young person to identify the opportunities.

"Drawing enables us not only to look but to see."

Julie Read, Artist

If they don't develop the initial work done in the research section, then the resolved work will be weak and when their portfolio is assessed they will score low in this area.

3. Contextual Awareness

In this section on context, it is now essential to explore other artists and/or designers that have used ideas of a similar nature, or maybe they use materials in a way that inspires your young person. Your young person needs to identify *what* it is about these artists that inspire them. It is not good enough to say 'I just like it'; *why* do they like it?

NOTHING happens in a vacuum, and that includes art.

Has your young person seen any exhibitions lately that have inspired them? Putting the gallery interpretation leaflet with their comments, thoughts, observations etc. into the sketchbook demonstrates that they:

- have attended
- are engaging in the wider art world and putting their own work into context, and
- are taking the opportunity to reflect on the work and WHY it interested them.

4. Resolved Work/Critical Judgement

The final element of this four-section formula is about how your young person is making choices and decisions along the way about what's good and what's not so good.

How well does your young person judge which ideas have the most potential to achieve their intended outcome? With a sketchbook full of ideas, models, and experiments, they must commit to creating a final piece for presentation, requiring careful choices.

Resolved work is usually a stand-alone piece/s. But the critical judgement and selection parts of stage 4 can be shown, if desired, in a sketchbook.

It's important for you and your young person to realise that they are already covering these elements in their school art and design curriculum, even if they aren't using the same language or aware that they are doing so.

You've likely come across various wording from different universities regarding portfolio expectations. If you and your young person understand that this illustration's content covers what universities want to see, how can you ensure it's thoroughly and explicitly included in the portfolio?

Digital Portfolios

Having discussed so far what a portfolio is, we'll now cover what is submitted for your application in the case of most universities and colleges.

There are exceptions, so please do research with your young person to find out which institutions still offer in-person, face-to-face interviews.

This will depend on whether a digital portfolio will be requested or not. If you are at all unsure, an email or phone call to admissions is the quickest way to gain clarity and peace of mind.

The digital portfolio is a file or files that digitally document the actual physical artwork. It doesn't need to be a portfolio where the artwork is created digitally, however, some students will create some artwork digitally just by the very nature of their chosen subject (graphic design, illustration for example).

Good, clear, well-lit photographs of the physical artwork are imperative to a successful digital portfolio. The digital photos should be a realistic representation of the actual piece of work in colour, tone and clarity of image.

From experience, a digital portfolio can make a weak actual portfolio appear much stronger. Likewise, a poor-quality digital portfolio can really reduce the quality of good work if the lighting and the quality of the images are poor and the layout and flow of the portfolio are haphazard.

Also choosing the work that shows the best flow of the process and projects is key to demonstrating the strength of the work.

Each institution has its own guidelines on how many pieces of artwork they wish to see. Therefore it will be necessary to adapt the digital portfolios to each of the universities' requirements.

Some universities are very specific about how many pieces of work they wish an applicant to submit, and this is often broken up into how many ideas, development, final and context (influential artists and designers) images that they wish to see in a portfolio.

Other universities just ask for a specific number of total images, and it's left open for interpretation what you "should" include.

There are pros and cons to both methods, and knowing which approach is required assists in planning and seeing where the gaps lie in the portfolio. If your young person has given themselves plenty of time to allow for the digital portfolio creation, then this isn't a problem, and gaps can be filled if guided adequately.

The format of what will be requested can often be available on the universities' websites. However many universities don't publish the details until the application has been made, and when they invite you to submit your portfolio.

Teachers may have experience of assisting students applying to certain universities and know what to expect. Do remember that these can and do change fairly frequently at some institutions.

There are also technical aspects to consider, such as if the universities wish to see portfolio images as a JPEG or a PDF file type; under a certain Megabytes (MB) in file size; or some may ask for images to be uploaded onto websites such as Tumblr or Flickr.

Therefore, having a knowledge of image types and file sizes is critical to ensure that your young person's images are accepted for submission, and their application isn't rejected before even being seen.

As you can see, it's critical early on that you and your young person gather this information for each institution, so that you're both aware of what will be requested, how and when.

Set Tasks and Additional Statement

A part of the selection process for some universities is to submit an additional set task following or prior to submitting a digital portfolio.

This is sometimes asked for along with a more tailored personal statement to that individual university, as the UCAS statement is generic, and the same UCAS statement is sent to each university choice.

There are no rules about which institutions ask for a set task, so please ensure your young person does their research as to what the process is where they're applying.

Architecture sometimes has this element to their process, although as I mentioned previously, there are some universities that don't ask for a portfolio at all for Architecture. Each is different; it is not limited to architecture, so please be prudent and get organised.

I hope that this Chapter provides clarity in understanding the process involved, but also the commitment that your young person needs to realise before they apply for art and design courses.

It's a competitive world, but certainly not impossible to enter. Some courses, such as fashion design and performance costume design, have only places for some 13 or 14 students – not just for UK students, but for ALL students.

It can be tempting for your young person to think "What's the point, I'll never get a place". However, I always advise my students that someone has to get those places, and it might as well be you.

It IS possible.

You can download a free spreadsheet that assists in organising application information in the resources area at www.portfolio-oomph.com/creativecareers.

Your Task

If this Chapter inspired just one action today, please let it be to download the above worksheet and start gathering information on the institutions your young person is applying to and what is required for the content of their application.

By visiting each university's website, your young person can start to populate the spreadsheet with the following information:

- When are the deadlines for the online application (UCAS or direct to the College)?

- What kind of digital portfolio does each university require?
- How many pieces of work does each university wish to see in the portfolio?
- Are there certain categories that their work needs to fit into based on the creative process?
- Which universities also do interviews?
- Are there set tasks/home assignments required?
- Is there a further statement required in addition to the UCAS statement?

I've found that having this information to hand in one place saves so much time and stress, rather than having to dig deep into the universities' websites each time you need the information. I'm also old-school and I find that printing these completed planning sheets out and pinning them somewhere in view also helps to ensure clarity.

This allows your young person more time to focus on being creative and doing what they love!

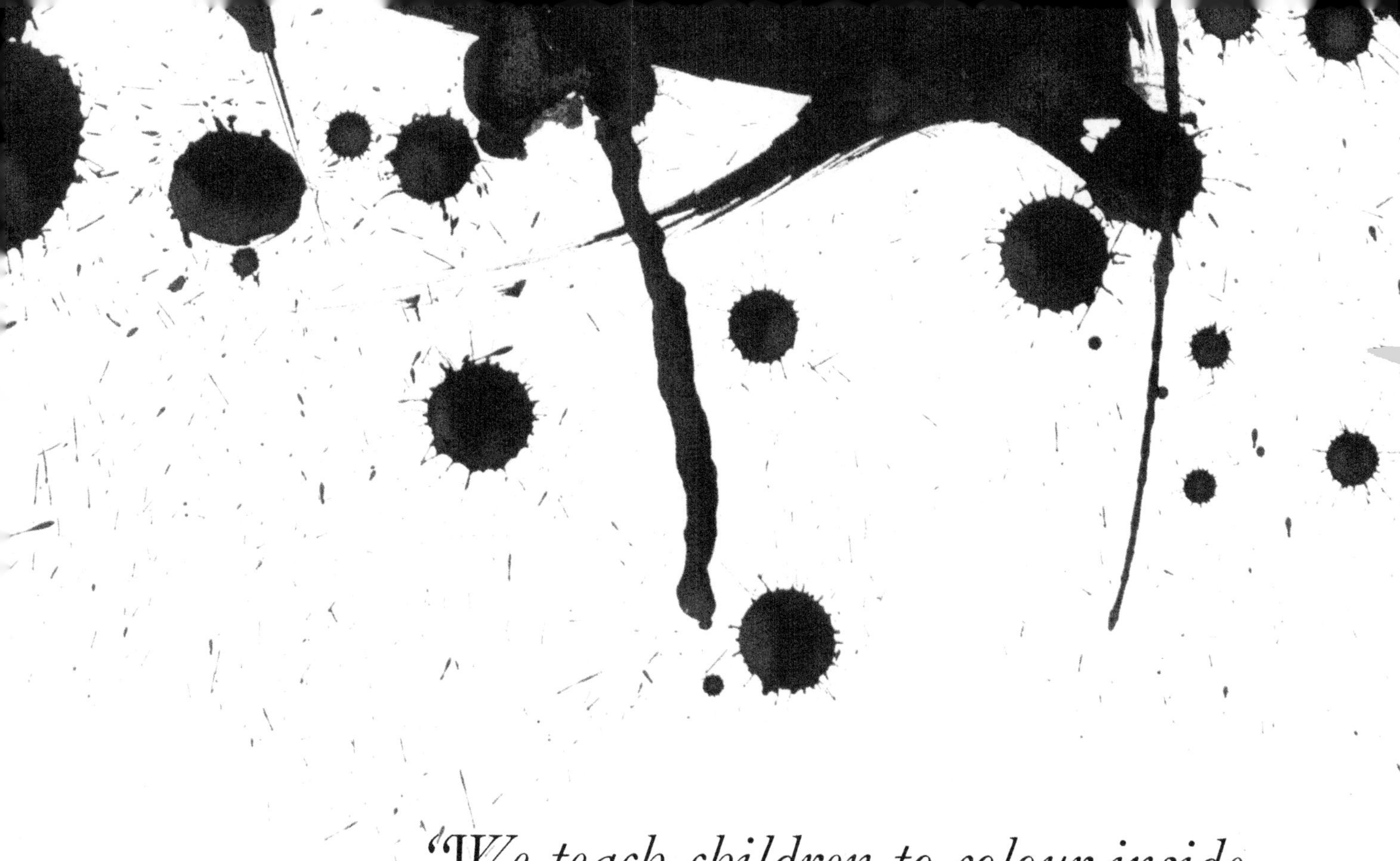

"We teach children to colour inside the lines and then expect adults to think outside the box."

Frank Sonnenberg, Author

7

How Will You Handle Interviews?

How Will You Handle Interviews?

7

If your young person has produced a cracking portfolio then they *may* be called for an interview.

Not all universities interview applicants. For some, the interview stage is after a pre-selection from your digital portfolio submission. If they like what they see then they will be asked to attend an interview – either online or in person.

The thought of interviews are pretty daunting, as not everyone is comfortable talking about their artwork – or even knows HOW to do it. It's quite unlike anything that your young person has probably done before, very different even to a job interview, where you're talking about yourself and your skills to do the job.

Talking about art and ideas and motivation can all seem very abstract, and – dare I say it – pretentious.

This is where having personal work in your portfolio really comes into its own. If all your young person has in their folio is work set by the teacher, that doesn't really light their fire, then it's very difficult to talk with enthusiasm.

Personally, I found the thought of going to an interview and having to big myself up terrifying when I was 19. I would never have guessed that my future career would be standing up in front of a room of students each day teaching, inspiring, mentoring. At 19, I was quite shy, quiet and didn't know how to blow my own trumpet.

I was also that student who didn't get a place at art college…in fact, three art colleges. I was gutted, as I thought my portfolio was great. The thing I didn't realise was that my portfolio said nothing about me and what I was interested in. And it showed quite clearly that my passion for art hadn't really been ignited.

I could draw and paint well technically, but the subjects I was drawing and painting about were dull, to be quite honest. I did paintings of poppy seed heads, flowers and shells, all because I didn't know what else to do. It was stuff we just had lying around at home; it showed!

When I was called to interview (everyone was interviewed in the 1990s as you took your portfolio with you), I was so timid and quiet that the interviewers got nothing out of me – no passion, no personality - at all. I had nothing to say about my work as it was so bland – how was I going to get them excited about my work if I wasn't even excited about it?

I naively came away thinking that they didn't talk much to me because my work gave them all the answers - I was SO wrong!

But I didn't discover this until I found myself begrudgingly repeating my Foundation Diploma to build a stronger portfolio, when – *thud (!)* – the penny finally dropped, my interests were broadened and my portfolio flourished.

Once my confidence grew, I secured a place at two colleges the following year and took up my place at Duncan of Jordanstone College of Art and Design in Dundee in 1991.

Now I am not saying that your young person needs to have a total personality transformation for their interview, if they are quiet and not so confident.

It takes all kinds of personalities to be creative – just look at all the personalities of successful artists and designers – and however quiet your young person may be, universities *are* interested in everyone.

Still, your young person needs to be able to pluck up the courage to talk about themselves and their work in some way that they feel comfortable in doing.

I find that engaging the student in the reflection process that we discussed in Chapter 6 is a powerful process in learning to communicate about their work.

By frequently thinking about and noting down what they're doing, what's working, what's challenging and possibly not working - this helps to build confidence with the language required to *talk* about their work in a way that they may be *asked* about at an interview.

Why Is an Interview Important?

When a student presents their portfolio, it's great to see what they have achieved.

I interviewed hundreds of students at Edinburgh College of Art, in person with their portfolios.

On some occasions a student presents a pretty mediocre portfolio. Sometimes, a student might have a great head on their shoulders, and it might be that they're not being encouraged in the best way, or their course isn't best aligned to their particular interests, for example.

By meeting the student, it can make a huge difference in determining whether or not they are good at what they do, but need more direction in a better way. Or, it may also be that they really aren't cut out for art or design at university. You will be surprised at how revealing an interview can be.

Things to do Before the Interview

Most interviews are quite relaxed and informal. As with job interviews, they are really designed to check that your young person is right for the course, but also that the course is right for them.

However, there are some things your young person should do to prepare.

Research

Make sure they've recently read about the university and the particular course for which they are applying, to ensure that they are fully informed.

Personal Statement

They should re-read their personal statement. I would also print a copy to have during the interview. This is so that they can refresh their memory about what they wrote. There's nothing worse than having written it, leaving it a few weeks or months, then being asked about something in the statement and drawing a blank, as if they never even wrote it (let's hope they did!).

Contact Other Applicants

If your young person knows of any students who've already applied to the same university and course, try to speak to them if they can. Universities should have a strict set of questions that they will ask everyone on a particular course to ensure that it is a level playing field for everyone. This gives each student the same opportunity to provide the same information to be assessed on fairly.

Know What is Happening in the World/Art World

Read a quality newspaper or magazine related to their subject – interviewers may ask for opinions on current affairs or developments in the field that your young person is applying to. Some examples of art-related magazines (or digital versions) that you can buy either online or at contemporary galleries nationwide would be *Art Review* (Fine art), *Studies in Photography, Sculpture and Selvedge* (Textiles).

Plan a Mock Interview

If your young person can have a teacher or tutor they're not familiar with to prepare a formal interview, it will give them an idea of what to expect.

I know it possibly seems unnecessary, but I did this the second time I applied, and it helped enormously.

To help your young person prepare well for the interview, you can download some example questions in the free PDF in the resources area www.portfolio-oomph.com/creativecareers.

During the Interview

Interviews can be really nerve wracking. However, it's important that your young person communicates their interest in the course to the interviewer/s – enthusiasm is key.

If they can take their time with questions – not to feel pressured to answer immediately, take a little while to develop their answers to avoid saying the first thing that comes into their head. It's okay to say, "I'll have to think about that" and then have a think and respond.

If they don't understand the question, they can say so. Interviewers don't expect applicants to know everything and will often prompt or rephrase a question if asked. There is often a very different language used in academia, and it's okay to ask for clarification.

Give full answers – this was my weakness. I assumed too much that my interviewer would understand me. The interviewer isn't telepathic and doesn't know what your young person has been through in their journey of creating their portfolio.

They are trying to find out about the INDIVIDUAL in every applicant, so if they can consider how to communicate their interests and passions, then that's a good starting point.

Listen to the interviewer – answer the questions asked rather than the ones they've prepared for.

Ask Some Questions

Always have your young person prepare some questions too. Try to find out the answers to them first by looking on their website or prospectus. If the university provides the answer to your question on the first page of their website or prospectus, don't ask this as the interviewers will presume they've not done any research about the university.

Have any questions written down on a piece of paper and consult it. It won't look like your young person is disorganised, I would say the opposite in fact; that they've given it some thought and that they'd like their burning questions answered.

Some good ones might be:

- How is the course assessed?
- What teaching methods are used?
- Do the tutors have exhibitions of their work that students can see?

If you or your young person can think of any more personal issues that you may want to discuss in the interview do make note of these so that you can discuss them if you get time.

My experience is that more and more students are requiring additional support needs to assist with their learning. Whilst this might not be a question that academic staff wish to answer, they can certainly point you in the right direction of where to get the answers that you're looking for – this might be the student support department.

Your young person must be prepared to talk about any of the work in their portfolio.

After the Interview

If your young person can write down the questions that they were asked and their responses to them, it would be helpful. It may be that they have more than one interview to do and to make improvements on how they responded would be worthwhile.

A Final Word

Encourage your young person to be themselves and not try to be what they think universities are looking for. Universities invest in them as individuals, valuing those who aren't afraid to express themselves. Your young person is great, creative, intuitive, and above all THEMSELVES!

"They always say time changes things, but you actually have to change them yourself."

Andy Warhol, Artist

8

You Got (or Didn't Get) the Offer. What's Next?

You Got (or Didn't Get) the Offer. What's Next?

8

HUGE congratulations are in order if you've arrived at this part of the book having completed the process of supporting your young person through applying to art and design courses at university. Now it's time to review potential offers and firm up your young person's plans.

Depending on where your young person has applied, they may have been scrutinised in their creative abilities, and it can feel very personal if the results aren't what they wanted or expected.

It's important that whatever result they achieve, the next decisions that they make remain fully informed. Some digging deep may be required. It's easy to get excited and feel flattered by receiving offers - any offers.

Likewise, it's easy to be blinkered and think that only an offer from your top university matters. Exciting opportunities could be missed if your young person is too focused on their top choice.

So it's beneficial if you can be active in helping your young person to have an open mind, and to consider the pros and cons of the situation. This was the case with Maisie, the daughter of a friend of mine, and who had a university choice that stood high above all the other courses that she applied for.

She wasn't offered a place there, unfortunately; however she did receive an offer from what was probably her least preferred choice!

There was much upset as she had achieved A grades in her school art. Weeks of deliberating and soul/ego-searching ensued, over whether to join a Foundation course with the aim to apply again to her top choice the following year, or to bite the bullet and take up the offer that she had. There are no guarantees either that by doing a Foundation course she would be successful.

There is no right thing to do - I will say that now. Maisie did choose to take the place at her least preferred option and is having the time of her life and regrets nothing.

So waiting and assessing your young person's options thoroughly is advisable, as is making more visits to the universities where they are holding offers.

Your young person will hear from their applications with one of the following:

An Unconditional Offer - this is if your young person is already qualified and their application has been successful.

A Conditional Offer - this is for students who are still to sit final school exams or college units and the results have not been confirmed. They may have predicted grades, and the offer from the university will give details of what the condition is that they have to meet in order to be eligible to take up the offer.

Unsuccessful - this notification is received when there are reasons to believe your young person is not working at a high enough level to be offered a place. Alternatively, it may be that they don't consider the course a good match for your young person. It may be due to not being qualified or the contents of their application (personal statement, portfolio, interview) scoring low in their assessment criteria.

If your young person has multiple offers, then huge congratulations are in order. This is no mean feat but now comes the difficult part of deciding which one to accept – we'll cover this.

If your young person doesn't have the offer/s that they wanted, then you're in the right place. This Chapter will advise and assist you in knowing what your young person's options are now and what you can do next.

Accepting an Offer

The hard work has been done! If your young person is holding more than one offer then it's crunch time to decide.

It might be a no-brainer with a clear 1st choice and the other courses were just back-ups/insurance choices.

However, if your young person really isn't sure which offer to take, then it's worth taking some time to consider their options well.

They might also find that they're in the position where they have an offer quite early from their most preferred choice and it's a long time waiting to hear from some of the other applications. This can be troublesome as pressure is felt to accept this early offer before all offers are in, as residential accommodation can be difficult to secure if they leave it too late.

This shouldn't really pose a problem, but it is always preferable to see where and how many offers your young person might get – there's nothing like being in demand!

Please be mindful of dates for confirming your young person's offers, and look out in the offer email for further information on completing your next steps.

If you or your young person are unsure about confirming their choice, then there is no harm in contacting the universities where offers are held, and asking if they can have a tour/see the departments to ask any further questions. Some universities have offer holder days to do exactly this.

Your young person will be able to register online for the event and they might also be asked to book some of the talks they're interested in to make sure they get a place on the day. Your young person needs to have received an offer, been invited and registered.

You and your young person may have visited already on Open Day as I recommended earlier on in the book. However, Open Days can often feel a bit misleading. Depending on the size of the institution, many of the students who are currently on the courses may have decided to work from home because of all the distractions. Therefore, you may not have had a realistic view of the actual experience.

If the universities that you have offers from don't have offer holder days, my recommendation would be to contact the universities that have made your young person's shortlist and see if there's a date and time when your young person can visit to speak to students, speak to staff and tour the workshops and studios on a normal working day.

As I mentioned in previous Chapters, I'm also a firm believer in gut instinct and intuition.

There may be other, more practical considerations, such as the cost of living in certain cities, accommodation pricing, and any special needs that your young person might require that pose limitations not only in the institution but the size of the institution, the size of the city, how far out of the city they may find the campus and just the general practicalities of living in the city for what can be three or four years.

Consideration also should be given to travelling home in the holidays and the practicalities of being a long way from home if your young person becomes homesick and feels the need to return more frequently.

If They Didn't Get Any Offers

First of all, don't panic! Your young person is likely to hear the results from their applications anytime between March and the end of April.

There are still opportunities after this time, which I'll explain.

UCAS Extra and Clearing

UCAS Extra is available to give applicants additional choices during the process of making their applications: if all 5 choices weren't used, if no offers were made to your young person, and if they don't wish to take up any of the offers that they've received. Please visit the UCAS website directly to find out more specifically whether your young person is eligible to use UCAS Extra and the dates when this is open for use.

UCAS Clearing is how universities fill any places they still have on their courses and opens in the summer – check the UCAS website for exact dates. There can be some amazing places still available during Clearing. However, this isn't something I would rely on, as it's very much dependent on the applications they receive and the standards each year.

If your young person didn't receive any offers (or any that they wanted to accept), didn't meet the conditions of an offer – grades for example, or is simply applying late for any reason, they may still be able to apply through Clearing.

I'll tell you a bit of my very own Clearing experience as a young, excited art student wanting to go off and explore the world of Art College.

Armed with my portfolio and NO preparation, I went off to Norwich School of Art (as it was called then) for an interview. I'd chosen this place as it seemed quite intimate, not the size of some of the large cities I'd visited such as Manchester and Leeds. I was so desperate to get into this school and I knew very little about the city, the institution or the reputation as it stood.

Had I done my research properly I would have known that it was a very competitive school to secure a place at. Not that this should have influenced my decision, but it could have saved a lot of upset as you will later find out.

As I mentioned earlier in the book, my interview was very uneventful and quick!

I'd worn my smartest clothes as my parents had advised. And I'd dropped in the name of my tutor who had studied with one of the interviewers as I thought this might help – Yay!

Nay!

I didn't get a place. I didn't ask for any feedback either.

I went to my 2nd choice college, as in those days your choices were sequential, and your application went through your choices 1 and 2 until you either were offered a place or got to the end with no offers!

Finally it went to Clearing – where as I previously explained, all the institutions with unfilled places are available for students to make an application to.

Having no accurate indication why I didn't obtain a place at Norwich, I went on to Humberside Polytechnic and did the same thing there – didn't say much, wore my smartest clothes and thought it went well too.

I didn't get a place there either - gutted.

I went through Clearing too at Farnham and surprise, surprise I didn't get a place there either!

Having asked for no feedback on my travels from any of these institutions, I had no idea why they weren't interested in me or my work. It wasn't based on my clothes being too smart I don't think! But I certainly didn't feel that comfortable in them, which, in hindsight didn't help, and didn't seem important beforehand.

And you know the rest – I repeated my Foundation Diploma and secured a place at two colleges the following year, and took up my place at Duncan of Jordanstone College of Art and Design in Dundee in 1991.

If your young person doesn't get into university or art college this year, please don't give them or yourself a hard time. *Applying to art college is very competitive.*

But having a considered plan about what they are going to do about it is essential.

Please congratulate your young person for applying, creating and presenting their portfolio. And if they had one, for attending what must have seemed quite a daunting task: the interview.

It might not seem like it right now, but having done all of these is a very good experience.

Some schools have this thing about "There are no losers – everyone's a winner". That's just not true, and your young person will be finding this out right now. Life is competitive, and we know as parents, that no one is going to hand anything to your young person on a plate just for trying. This is just the beginning.

But it does take some experience to learn this, and it's a hard pill to swallow at ages 17 or 18.

So what are the options and what are they going to do?

Options:

[a] Cry and give up

[b] Cry, give up and never set foot inside a gallery or look at art again. I HATE ART!

[c] Dunno, see what happens…..

[d] Take a year out to travel and apply again with the same portfolio next year

[e] Take a year out to travel and work in sketchbooks whilst away, apply again with additional work

[f] Get a job instead, don't apply again

[g] Take a year out to work and apply again with the same portfolio next year
[h] Take a year out to work, attend some evening classes and add to their portfolio to apply again next year
[i] Apply for a portfolio building/foundation course and apply again next year with a revised portfolio
[j] Take up a place on another course that they're also keen to do

Many of these options are right for many applicants.

University or art school isn't for everyone, and it would be wrong for me to say to your young person that they must try again, only harder and they will get in. They might not.

They might not have the ambition or finances or commitment to do that.

They need to decide, with you, if their ambition to study art or design at university is strong enough to justify spending another year, in terms of time and money, reapplying.

However, under no circumstance do I suggest that either [d] or [g] is a good option.

Why?

Because there is no point applying with the same portfolio if it didn't get your young person a place this time – it's unlikely to win a place next time. If they apply with the same portfolio to the same college, the portfolio assessors will expect to see new artwork created in the year since – and often they will remember a portfolio, I assure you.

So, if your young person has decided that they are really destined to go to university to study art or design like I was, then they have to try again.

If you can support your young person to help them improve their portfolio by staying on at school or attending evening classes or a Foundation course, then that is great.

I'd recommend taking the following actions to get on point and re-start the process with as much information as possible.

Action Step 1: Get Proper Feedback.
The best way is to email the university from where your young person was rejected.

Admissions is usually the first port of call.

Your young person should ask them what the procedure is for obtaining feedback from their application and DO IT.

Action Step 2: Get Well-Informed to Take Action.
Spend a little time – and I mean weeks, not minutes – thinking about what the feedback is really saying. There will probably be notes made in connection to different aspects of your young person's application and their

portfolio. So, what elements made up their application?

Exam results/qualifications – This may sound obvious, but is your young person qualified for the course they applied to? Only very occasionally a student can be offered a place without the academic grades IF their portfolio is out-of-this-world exceptional. However, this is not common. If your young person is waiting for exam results, this is a different matter. And if an offer is made, it will be on the condition that you make the grades necessary in the letter of offer (a conditional offer).

Personal statement – There might be comments about this on your young person's notes, but usually feedback is given on the portfolio and application holistically.

Portfolio – This is the big hurdle; however it's the part that you'll receive most useful information about if feedback is requested.

Your young person is likely to receive a numerical score that shows the areas that the universities assess in all applicants' portfolios, and where they scored in each area. There won't be specific information about projects and personal work in the feedback.

In the resources area at www.portfolio-oomph.com/creativecareers, you can download a PDF that provides insight into the feedback process, including an example of the scores a student, Kirsty, received on her portfolio over four years of applying.

When Kirsty found that she had three times been rejected from her no. 1 course, she realised that even though she had feedback on her portfolio every year and how it scored, what she was missing was advice on HOW to take positive steps to improve.

And that is the key - knowing what the feedback actually means in relation to your work, and what needs to happen for your young person to nudge those scores up.

Each year her scores became increasingly lower and lower; as such, her confidence sank to rock bottom. Not because she wasn't capable, but because she'd lost sight of the process and lacked the support, as she'd already left college.

This is in comparison to the final scores she received on the year she was accepted - when she was adequately supported to make these improvements with focus and clarity.

Moving forward, it's no good to apply again with the same knowledge. Your young person will likely get the same results. That's why it's important to ask for feedback and to interpret it accurately.

There may be short notes in each area that they've scored on. They could be minimal, and this could be quite difficult to interpret into any meaningful feedback.

If this is the case, please ask your young person's art teacher to help translate it.

The notes will be about the quality of the work, and some examples would be: ideas/concepts, research/investigation, drawing skills, developmental work, resolved work (critical judgement and selection), presentation, influences/contextual awareness and sketchbooks.

Whatever is written in relation to each of these categories, your young person will need to take this on board and ask themselves, "How could I have done better?"

They might not know what they could have done better, and their teacher might not know either. But it's useful to seriously think about it. Over the summer is probably a good time to start – not once school starts back (if they're returning) or if they're taking a job on for a year, as they are likely to forget and then get caught up in other things.

Interview – This might have severely let your young person down. Of course, the interviewers realise that nerves can be difficult to manage, so comments don't usually relate to that unless it's been a particularly bad interview.

Usually, comments relating to the interview would be about attitude, lack of knowledge of the specialist subject that your young person is applying to, a seeming lack of commitment, or caring about future artistic career, lack of engagement in the creative process, inability to communicate about the work in their portfolio etc.

Once your young person has this information and can gauge where the gaps lie in the portfolio and interview if they've had one, then a plan of action can be formed to reapply next year if they wish.

Action Step 3: Make a Plan.

Seeking advice on HOW your young person is going to make improvements on this year's application is essential if they are planning to apply again next year.

They may be taking up a place on their backup plan at further education – hopefully they made one (as advised in Chapter 1)!

If this is the case I would advise they need to remain focused and aware that the competitive nature of applying to art and design courses remains, even when a student has done a Foundation Diploma course or HNC/D.

If for some reason your young person didn't apply with a backup plan to further education colleges, then do still look into this and apply immediately if they are still taking applications.

By enrolling on a Foundation Diploma course, your young person may find that they are just 1 of over 100 students - as they can be large groups each year that are accepted.

When faced with a complete change of approach from school and that of A level art to more experimental risk-taking art, this can come with its own problems, in that a student can feel like nothing they have done is "good", and that they are out of their depth with how to see the value in this new approach.

Seeking 1:1 support would also be a preferred option, depending on the structure/duration. It provides an individual plan and approach, with personal feedback and adequate time to discuss your young person's goals and concerns.

We talked about Dyson early on in this book, in Chapter 3 on creativity. I truly believe that if a student really wants to pursue a career in the creative industries, then it's a matter of just trying again - but with more knowledge.

This quote from Sir James Dyson summarises much of what I've discussed through this book, and I hope that my message is clear.

> "I made 5,127 prototypes of my vacuum before I got it right. There were 5,126 failures. But I learned from each one. That's how I came up with a solution. So I don't mind failure. I've always thought that school children should be marked by the number of failures they've had. The child who tries strange things and experiences lots of failures to get there is probably more creative."

> "We're taught to do things the right way. But if you want to discover something that other people haven't, you need to do things the wrong way. Initiate a failure by doing something that's very silly, unthinkable, naughty, dangerous. Watching why that fails can take you on a completely different path. It's exciting, actually. To me, solving problems is a bit like a drug. You're on it, and you can't get off."

The main piece of advice I can give is for your young person not to give up if it's truly what they want in life.

CONCLUSION

You've made it to the end!

And by doing so you have significantly increased your young person's chances of success. However, no amount of knowledge outperforms taking bold action, and that is what I invite you to do next.

For your young person, making a fully informed application to university for art and design courses is the first step in the journey of creative self-discovery. And for you as a parent, I commend you for doing the thorough research to support them to follow their hearts.

To summarise, we've split the book into the practical and technical aspects of making the application; what needs to be done, how and when. With clarity and understanding, the journey and the options for your young person should now be clearer with the overview of this bigger picture.

However, the biggest learning that I hope you and your young person will thoroughly embrace is the attention to an understanding of what creativity is and the mindset required for success.

Having clarity of the process required from the outset puts your young person at a distinct advantage. This enables them to get started early and to ensure that the process is fully explored, therefore providing strong evidence in ALL areas of the assessment criteria from the universities. Not only will this result in your young person feeling able to create their best portfolio, but it will also enable them to feel confident with the work, and ultimately being able to talk about it at an interview.

Following the steps in this book and making a well-structured plan means your young person will know where they currently are, where they want to be, and most importantly, *how* they are going to get there.

My opinion is that if your young person can adopt the risk taking, the notion of failing, resilience and persistence, then they will not only excel with their current portfolio and creative work, but they will hit the ground running and make the most of every opportunity that comes their way in life.

They will be *fearless!*

And this is the perfect way to stop in the tracks those well known traits of the creative – that of procrastination and perfectionism. These can be deal breakers when the clock is ticking towards the application deadlines.

Your creative person has the potential and power to change lives, and I don't mean this lightly. I believe that creativity can unlock profound insights into the human experience, and foster deeper connections with ourselves and others, bringing a sense of fulfilment and happiness to life.

Not to mention the human issues that can be addressed through art and design, and may significantly improve the quality of life and that of humanity's future.

I've spoken to parents who, in their own words:

> **"...we were in kind of desperation, a bit of panic, quite a lot of anxiety, and we just really didn't know what to do."**

If you also felt like this at the start of reading this book, I hope that those feelings have subsided, and you now feel empowered with the knowledge to get the job done.

The best part is that now, not only do you have the steps required in supporting your young person through making an application to university or art school, but in the deeper understanding of the kind of attitudes and mindsets required to make a successful life in the creative world.

American novelist, E.L. Doctorow once said,

> **"Writing a novel is like driving a car at night. You can see only as far as your head-lights, but you can make the whole trip that way."**

In this sense, you can substitute writing a novel for creating art, and the meaning of the quote still applies.

You don't have to see where you're going (the whole creative journey), you don't have to see your destination (the final artwork), you just have to see two or three feet ahead of you (make a start, take baby steps).

If you've not already downloaded the additional resources to complement the content in this book, please do so at www.portfolio-oomph.com/creativecareers and learn more! Learn more about how Portfolio Oomph can support you in making your young person's dreams a reality. These resources will cement the themes in this book and provide some practical opportunities to take bold action.

Your young person will shine through their art, and I hope this book has helped you both to light the road, just two or three feet ahead!

If this book has helped you in one small way, then it's done its job.

That might even be that your young person decides that they don't have the grit, determination or even the desire that's required to give an art and design application its best shot.

And that's okay. Something else will give them that opportunity to shine.

But of course, I'm hoping that it's really lit a fire in yours and the belly of your young person to "go get it" (as my tutor Tony Currell said to me on my second year applying - and I did).

To go for what they dream of. What are they waiting for?!

Incidentally, all the information in this book is also relevant to mature learners who may be wishing to return to education. Maybe it's you?

Every year I take on a small number of students whom I mentor, assisting them in implementing the ideas, and more, within this book. We work together closely to grow confidence, explore creativity, and gain great clarity to produce that killer portfolio for success at art school.

If you wish to find out more about working with me, please act now and get in touch.

I'd love to know how you're feeling and what takeaways you have from this book.

Please connect with me on social media:

Facebook: https://www.facebook.com/portfolio.oomph
Instagram: https://www.instagram.com/portfoliooomph
Pinterest: https://www.pinterest.co.uk/portfoliooomph
X: https://x.com/portfoliooomph
Youtube: https://www.youtube.com/@Portfoliooomphfolioadvice
LinkedIn: https://www.linkedin.com/in/julieread-oomph

"Get comfortable with being uncomfortable."

Julie Read, Artist

REFERENCES

Franken, R. E., Human Motivation, 3rd edn., Brooks/Cole Publishing Company, 1993.

Lucas, B., 'Creative Thinking in Schools Across the World: A Snapshot of Progress in 2022', 2022, https://www.researchgate.net/publication/364360090_Creative_thinking_in_schools_across_the_world (accessed 16 July 2024).

Prospects [website], Jisc, https://www.prospects.ac.uk/job-profiles/browse-sector/creative-arts-and-design, (accessed 16 July 2024).

Scott, E., 'Arts and Creative Industries: The Case for a Strategy', UK Parliament, 2022, https://lordslibrary.parliament.uk/arts-and-creative-industries-the-case-for-a-strategy, (accessed 16 July 2024).

Will Robots Take My Job? [website], https://willrobotstakemyjob.com, (accessed 16 July 2024).

World Economic Forum, 'The Future of Jobs Report 2023', World Economic Forum, 2023, https://www.weforum.org/publications/the-future-of-jobs-report-2023, (accessed 16 July 2024).

TESTIMONIALS

Anna Campbell-Jones, *Interior Design Consultant, TV presenter on BBC Scotland's Home of the Year.*

"I can only applaud this invaluable publication. It celebrates creativity, individuality and the necessary accompanying discomfort. So, paradoxically, this should be a comfort to anyone who reads it, whether prospective student or concerned parent/caregiver."

Dawn Gavin, *Professor and Dean of Undergraduate Studies at the School of the Art Institute of Chicago (SAIC)*

"Julie offers straightforward, practical advice that will not only prepare prospective students to pursue an arts-related degree but also provide valuable insights into how their educational journey can lead to a meaningful career in the creative arts and cultural industries."

Susan M. Coles, *Artist and Arts, Creativity and Educational Consultant*

"Julie's book acts as a compassionate guide, offering genuine knowledge and insights that empower you to support your young person during this critical phase of their lives.

With her informed and authentic approach, Julie ensures you are well-equipped to help them make informed decisions about their future in visual art education."

John Brown, *Course Organiser and Lecturer, Edinburgh College of Art - University of Edinburgh*

"This is a super-helpful and engaging book. The writing sparks off the page as Julie's personal experience is used very effectively to give clear information to help demystify art school applications and many aspects of creativity."

Nicola Smith, *Parent*

"Julie's book is full of invaluable information and guidance for those of us supporting our young people through the process of applying to study art. Her knowledge and understanding of both the process and how to support during the process of preparing a successful portfolio is second to none."

Bridget Frost, *Parent*

"The book is brilliant, an amazing resource. This book will be a lifeline to so many students and their supporters. What's more, it keeps the joy. It's incredibly exciting when someone has enough courage to follow their passion, but now, at last, it can be a little less terrifying too!"

Lily Burgess, *Student*

"Julie's advice and wisdom were an incredible help and really gave me hope. The contents of this book quite literally turned my life around."